DR. DARLINGTON AKAISO

FARMING WITH GUNS

A nation short on time and long on need

Publication data on file with National Library and Archives Canada

ISBN trade paperback 978-0578811833
ISBN: 0578811839

Published by Soyounique Publishers
www.soyounique.ca

CONTENTS

DISCLAIMER

All the work and opinions expressed herein are those of the author alone. They do not represent the opinion of any of the establishments with which the author is associated. Hence, no other party should be attributed to any errors of the fact of any kind related to this publication.

ABOUT THE AUTHOR

Dr. Darlington Akaiso is an academic scholar. He has written numerous books on global leadership studies. For over twenty years, he has worked in risk management, resilience planning, and international development. He has also taught in various capacities at the Northeastern University, University of Manitoba, Seneca College, Trent University in Canada, and the University of the West Indies in the Caribbean. He earned his bachelor's degree in Information Technology/Informatics from York University, Toronto, Canada, his master's degree in Management Information Systems from the University of Illinois-Springfield, USA, and his doctorate in Leadership from Franklin Pierce University, New Hampshire, USA. He is also an alumnus of the Massachusetts Institute of Technology (MIT), USA, and Harvard Kennedy School, Cambridge, MA, USA.

ABOUT THE BOOK

Across Nigeria, Christians are dying:

The Fulani herdsmen's invasion into peaceful communities of Nigeria has created a disturbing pattern of death and desecration; to this day none of the culprits have been brought to justice. Under the guise of an ancient livestock herding tradition, this group of people wage a war against the Christian population of the entire country. To protect their livestock, cattle farmers have graduated from using sticks, daggers and clubs to using sophisticated, brutal weapons like double-barrel shotguns and AK-47s.

Scholars the world over have been connecting this rise in violence to the Boko Haram insurgency, which has waged since 2009. Others wonder if this is a secret agenda aimed at wiping out non-Islamic populations in order to spread Islam to the conquered territories.

In this harrowing investigation, Dr. Darlington Akaiso asks the questions no one else is willing to ask.

- Why are Christian churches being targeted by the Fulani herdsmen?
- Could this be an ethnic cleansing, with Christians as the primary target?
- Can anything be done to stop the brutal murder of innocent Christians?
- How did guns in the first place make its way to the grazing farmlands of Nigeria?

FULANI HERDSMEN: HOW (WHY) GUNS FOUND ITS WAY TO THE FARMS

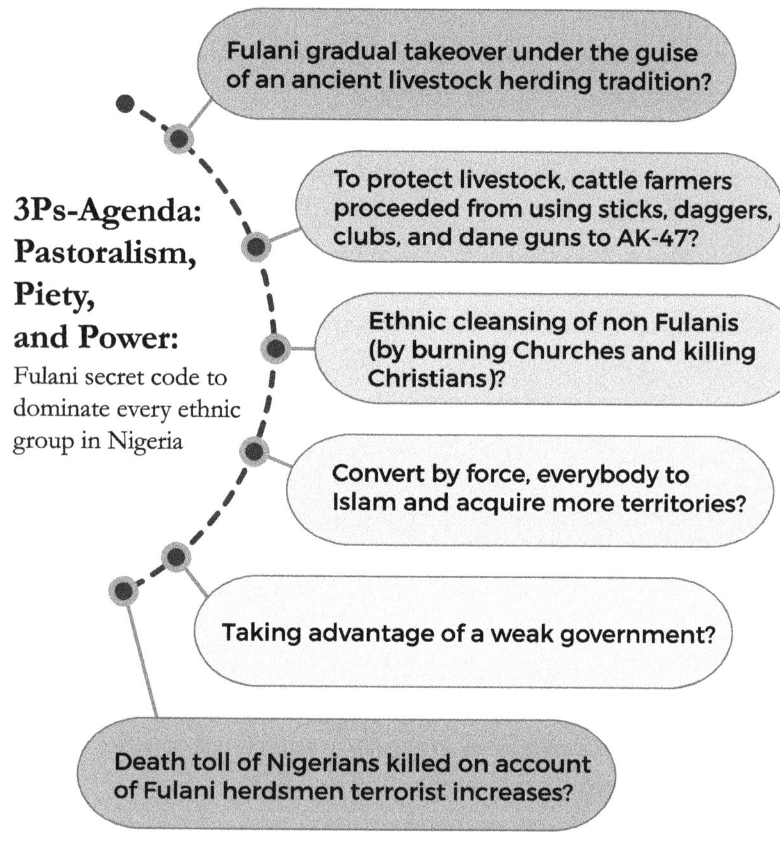

FULANI HERDSMEN: HOW (WHY) GUNS FOUND ITS WAY TO THE FARMS

3Ps-Agenda: Pastoralism, Piety, and Power:
Fulani secret code to dominate every ethnic group in Nigeria

- No Fulani herdsmen culprit have been arrested or brought to justice?
- Fulani herdsmen learned from Boko Haram how to use insurgency to cripple the government?
- Fulani herdsmen learned from Boko Haram how to reveal the system's inherent vulnerabilities?
- Fulani herdsmen learned from Boko Haram how to defy security measures?
- Fulani herdsmen learned from Boko Haram how to move arms and ammunition to their targeted places?
- Fulanis counter reaction when Kanuris rise to prominence in any administration?

FULANI HERDSMEN: HOW (WHY) GUNS FOUND ITS WAY TO THE FARMS

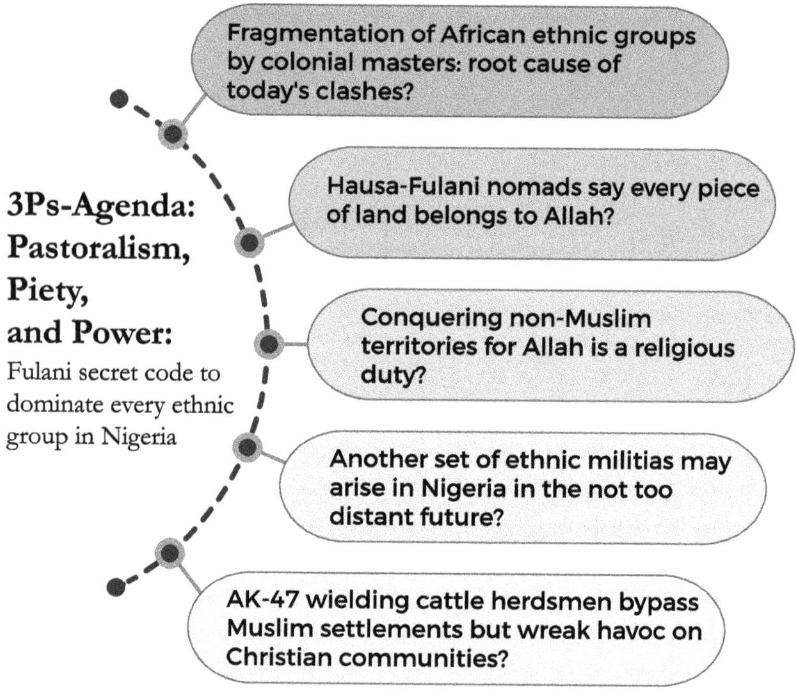

3Ps-Agenda: Pastoralism, Piety, and Power:
Fulani secret code to dominate every ethnic group in Nigeria

- Fragmentation of African ethnic groups by colonial masters: root cause of today's clashes?
- Hausa-Fulani nomads say every piece of land belongs to Allah?
- Conquering non-Muslim territories for Allah is a religious duty?
- Another set of ethnic militias may arise in Nigeria in the not too distant future?
- AK-47 wielding cattle herdsmen bypass Muslim settlements but wreak havoc on Christian communities?

PREFACE

Religion and ethnicity in Nigeria go hand in hand. This is not because Nigerians are very holy regarding their religious beliefs. Still, the fact is that major ethnic groups in the country see religion as a symbol of their identity. Therefore, deemphasizing the religion of a group tends to tantamount to taking away their ethnic presence, especially in the face of the inter-ethnic struggle for supremacy. Many crises in Nigeria do not occur in isolation of ethnic and religious underpinnings - even when they are sparked and escalated by certain factors that profoundly resemble immediate cause, they are mostly fueled by various religious and ethno-sectional suspicion. In the study of crises and their escalation, recent Fulani herdsmen clashes with the indigenes of various communities in Nigeria could easily be juxtaposed with other conflicts caused by ethnoreligious struggles that turn out to form the hallmark of Nigeria's bloodshed history.

Why did Fulani militants begin to enact wanton terrorism on other Nigerian ethnicities following the year the Boko Haram Islamic sect turned violent? The pattern and mode of Fulani herdsmen's belligerent operations could show that their militancy is just a quick response to Boko Haram terrorism, which rides on the back of the Kanuri ethnic agenda. Before the transition of Boko Haram from a seemingly benign Islamic sect to one of the deadliest terrorist groups in the world, Kanuri did not have a militancy system to help drive their ethnic schema in a pluralistic Nigerian state just like the Yoruba's O'odua Peoples' Congress (OPC); Igbo's Movement for the Actualization of the Sovereign State of Biafra (MASSOB), and the Ijaw's Niger-Delta militants. It was after the Nigerian police, in 2009, murdered Muhammed Yusuf, a Kanuri and the leader of Boko Haram, accompanied with ensued reprisals that sparked events leading to the transformation of Boko Haram to a ready apparatus for the Kanuri to use in avenging the death of their kinsmen, as well as seeking to address the disproportionate distribution of resources and opportunities in the country.

Again, why did Fulani militancy not spur by OPC, MASSOB, Niger-Delta militants, or something else but instead came on the heel of the Kanuri's Boko Haram movement? The Fulani herdsmen militancy could have been triggered by some other factors against the sedentary agricultural population long before the rise of Boko Haram terrorism in 2009. For centuries, herdsmen-farmers conflicts existed, although on a lighter scale. Then why did Fulani herdsmen turn militant following the Boko Haram uprising? Could it be that Fulani herdsmen would not have gone genocidal if the Fulani-Kanuri's battle for supremacy that commenced at the early turn of the 19th century did not come to the front burner?

Yes! The primary reason for the bloody Fulani herdsmen's attacks in recent times could remotely be traced to the enthronement of the Sokoto Caliphate over Hausa states by the Fulani, which was led by Uthman Dan Fodio and his son, Mohammed Bello, in the first quarter of the 19th century. After the Fulani jihadists defeated the Hausa kings, the North was then opened for Caliphacy that aspired to override all subsisting structures set in place by Habe traditions. The emerging situation later placed the Fulani ethnics on top of the Islamic religious, economic, and socio-political structures of the Northern system. At the same time, the Kanuri played second fiddle role even though Kanuri's Old Kanem-Bornu empire enjoyed centuries of Islamic civilization long before the establishment of Sokoto Caliphate in the 19th century.

It was actually the resistance of the Fulani expansionism by the Kanuri led by Muhammed Al-Kanemi that resulted in the existence of two Islamic power blocs in the North – that is, the Sokoto Caliphate spanning from the Northwest to the North-central and the Old Bornu Empire in the Northeast controlled by the Kanuri. With two powerful Islamic blocs existing side by side, hostility becomes inevitable, thus throwing the two blocs into stiff struggles for religious, cultural, socio-political, and ideological supremacy. The Fulani still manages to have an edge. When the Boko Haram uprising began in 2009, it becomes natural for the Fulani to suspect Kanuri of waging their version of Jihad through Boko Haram to take over the dominance of the North and beyond. As a matter of fact, the Salafist views held by Boko Haram condemning the Western lifestyle as impious coupled with their overt intention of establishing a Caliphate in Nigeria was a clear message to the Fulani, signaling to them a possible shift in the domination of the Northern system from Sokoto Caliphate to Bornu axis. Therefore, the only mechanism available for a violent reaction or what could be passed as ethnic militia to help halt the trend and maintain the status quo remains the Fulani herdsmen.

The major consideration in this work is that the Fulani in Nigeria exists with an age-long agenda that combine the "3Ps" of Pastoral, Piety, and Power interests. The agenda, which is guided by an unwritten code, does not glorify subservience. It is in the Fula secret code to seek dominance over other ethnicities in Nigeria; hence, it would not have been possible for the Fulani to sit back and watch a historic archrival as Kanuri bringing up an ethnic militia to scatter and reset the subsisting power equation to the disfavor of the Fulani. As Kanuri began to use Boko Haram in extending their influence from the Northeast towards North-central Nigeria, the Fulani responded by militarizing pastoralism to contain Kanuri's Boko Haram to their Northeast domain. Despite their background of rivalry, both militant groups do not attack each other but show preemption by taking their aggression on Christian or non-Muslim ethnic minorities. Observing the Fulani herdsmen attack pattern specifically, one would find out that their operations center predominantly in Benue, Plateau, Kaduna, Nasarawa, Taraba, Adamawa, and Kogi, Ondo, Enugu, Edo, and other states. Ostensibly, as a reaction against cattle rustling and the quest for grazing space, their moves have been observed to go with Islamic agenda and power ambition undercurrents. For instance, the Fulani, through their various platforms such as Myetti Allah Kautal Hore, Tabital Pulaaku Nigeria Chapter, Myetti Allah Cattle Breeders Association (MACBAN), and other socio-cultural groupings likely to be mentioned in this book, have been very vociferous in their support for passing into law the Open Grazing Bill, which would enable them to establish cattle colonies anywhere outside their northern domain. Such moves have been widely suspected of going with the intent of grabbing lands for the Fulani and as well as aiding them to entrench their system all over Nigeria.

The 3Ps have clearly been manifested as the Kanuri militants aroused the Fulani to adopt a protectionist approach by around 2010 while keeping an eye on the presidency; they further got motivated by Boko Haram getaways from many of their atrocities against the government and the law. Hence the Fulani militants had to gang up against a Nigerian government headed by Dr. Goodluck Jonathan, a Southern Christian. In 2015, when they eventually produced Muhammadu Buhari as the president whose mother is of Kanuri ethnicity, the Fulani's reaction swung against Kanuri characters' sudden rise in the national politics under Buhari's government, thus creating the need to offset the political equation once more. It seems the Fulani militancy has paid off as almost all the security structure and the Fulani dominate critical positions in the second tenure of Buhari presidency. But why are the herdsmen still killing as at the time of this writing? There is more to this narrative as we open pages and chapters of this book.

CHAPTER ONE

INTRODUCTION: FROM HERDSMEN-FARMERS CLASHES TO ETHNO-RELIGIOUS EXPANSIONIST WARFARE

All over the world, pastoralism is one common enterprise that goes with conflicts either between the pastoralists and the sedentary agriculturalists or amongst the pastoralists themselves. As far as livestock herding is concerned, no place in the world lack records of violent confrontations. History is replete with herding-induced crises all over the world. For instance, between 1870 and 1920, over 50 deaths were reportedly recorded in armed conflicts known as Sheep and Cattle Wars in the Western United States. These wars were fought between the shepherds and the cattlemen over rights to grazing land. These wars claimed both human lives and livestock from Texas and Arizona to other territories in Wyoming and Colorado. In Argentina and certain parts of Latin America, the vaqueros also conflicted with the corn farmers. The Bedouins were known to have regularly entered into struggles with other land inhabitants in Mid-East Asia as they tried to acquire grazing space. In South Sudan, Africa, cattle raiding became a traditional practice among the pastoral communities, notably amongst the Nuer, Dinka, and Murle ethnic groups[1]. On record, all of these activities often threw the pastoralists into crisis. In Somalia, where the livestock industry generates about 40% of its GDP and 80% of its foreign exchange[2], cases of violence between the cattle herders and the agriculturalists are numerous. This common experience of pastorally induced crises is common and natural because social life, based on social theory as stressed by Ugwumba Egbuta, is a competition and focuses on distributing resources and power that are not evenly endowed by nature[3].

The so-called Fulani herdsmen conflicts with farmers in Nigeria are not entirely different in origin from the commonplace crises emanating from pastoralism across the world. However, it is the economic, religious, political, environmental, and social factors together with the milieu of times that give the herders-farmers crisis in Nigeria its uniqueness. With the perennial ethnoreligious problems creeping into the normal tension between the pastoralists and the agriculturalists, the conflicts have become deadliest, eclipsing the existing records left behind by the world history the herders-farmers disputes.

It is worthy of note that conflicts did not often characterize the pastoralists-agriculturalists relationship in Nigeria. There were moments of cooperation too. In pre-colonial times, Fulani herders used to exchange some of their animal products with farmers for grains, thus supplementing each respective group's diets[4]. According to Davidheiser and Luna (2008), in the pre-colonial era, the subsistence and small-surplus peasant modes of production of Fulani herders and West African farmers were often intertwined in a mutually beneficial fashion[5]. As noted by Charles Frantz, competition and conflict between Fulani herdsmen and farmers "were often limited because of small human population pressures, periodic droughts, and an epidemic of cattle disease[6]." The colonial-era would come with policies that would make available resources more scarce, thus increasing competition and conflicts. Amongst such policies were flexible property rights that had been an important historic adaptive strategy in the Sahel, especially for Fulani[7]. In this connection, van den Brink, Bromley, and Chavas (1995) pointed out that "exclusive property regimes had repeatedly resulted in the 'overuse' of the resource base, amplification of adverse effects of drought periods, and increased conflicts between nomads and farmers, among nomadic groups, and within a nomadic group[8]."Again, colonialism brought new medical knowledge and practices to West Africa, and both the human and the cattle population rose greatly, increasing competition for resources[9]. As noted by J.D. Unruh, "land-use conflicts... increase as degradation of rangelands, growing populations, and greater pressures on these areas to produce food, cause increase competition for land and water resources[10]." This trend would continue well into the post-colonial era where the articulation of the modes of production continued, and many of the other processes such as urbanization, demographic pressure, and increased influence of a global market economy continued, decreasing available pasture land and increasing competition for natural resources in West Africa[11].

The violent confrontation between the Fulani nomads and the sedentary agriculturalists remains a recurring issue in the post-colonial era. Over a period, the Fulani have engaged in fighting with other local groups, specifically, the Jukun, Eggon, and Tiv communities. The disputes with these communities were mostly focusing on land disputes, though religious concerns also fueled the violence[12]. Fulani's contributions to those communal feuds mostly came either as initiation or reprisal for hostilities[13]. Casualties on both sides were on a minimal scale until the 2010s, especially around 2015, when the number of casualties caused by crises rose to an alarmingly high rate. In 2014 alone, the Fulani herdsmen militants became responsible for 1,229 deaths, which placed them at number four on the list of the deadliest terror groups compiled by the Global Terrorism Index[14]. The Fulani militants only trailed the Taliban, the Islamic State, and Boko Haram.

The sudden switch from crude weapons such as sticks, daggers, clubs, and dane guns to more sophisticated arms like double-barrel guns and AK47 rifles has dramatically changed Fulani's character and pattern of a violent attack on rival groups. Since the review period, their offensive has moved away from mere reprisals and quest to secure temporary grazing land to ethnic cleansing and Islamic jihad. Most victims of Fulani herdsmen militancy are indigenous Christian farmers - including non-farmers. In recent times, herders' attacks have become fatal in non-Fulani dominated domains in Benue, Southern Kaduna, Plateau, Nasarawa, Taraba, Kogi, while extending their onslaught to southern states like Ondo, Enugu, Edo, Anambra, and a few other States. Fulani militants, as observed, have equally become more intensive and reckless in brutality. Thcy allegedly rape women and kidnap for ransom too. Most times, their reasons for the attack are unfounded. For example, the Fulani militants reportedly gave no excuse following their murder of 17 indigenes of Gonan Rogo village in the Kajuru Local Government Area on Tuesday, 12th May 2020, while the Covid-19 lockdown was still in force. Indeed, the Southern Kaduna Peoples Union (SOKAPU) Nigeria confirmed this in a press statement that "no fewer than 17 persons were murdered in cold blood for no reason by persons who the villagers identified as Fulani[15]." SOKAPU Nigeria further described the attack as an "unrelenting massacre and ethnic cleansing[16]."

A careful look at the composition of persons killed in the Gonan Rogo attack exposes an intent geared at ethnic cleansing. The militants, from about 11:45 p.m. on 11th May to the early hours of 12th May 2020, murdered a baby, children, and adults. The list of persons killed, including their various ages, is presented below:

1.	Mailafiya Dallatu	70 years
2.	Yari Dallatu	60 years
3.	Na'omi Yari	57 years
4.	Blessing Yari	9 years
5.	Paul Bawa	18 years
6.	Rahila Paul	25 years
7.	John Paul	6-months
8.	Jonathan Yakubu	35 years
9.	Sheba Jonathan	25 years
10.	Revelation Jonathan	9 years
11.	Rejoice Jonathan	6 years
12.	Patience Jonathan	15 years
13.	Biyayya Lucky	25 years
14.	Asan'alo Magaji	32 years
15.	Yayo Magaji	13 years
16.	Agei Magaji	8 years

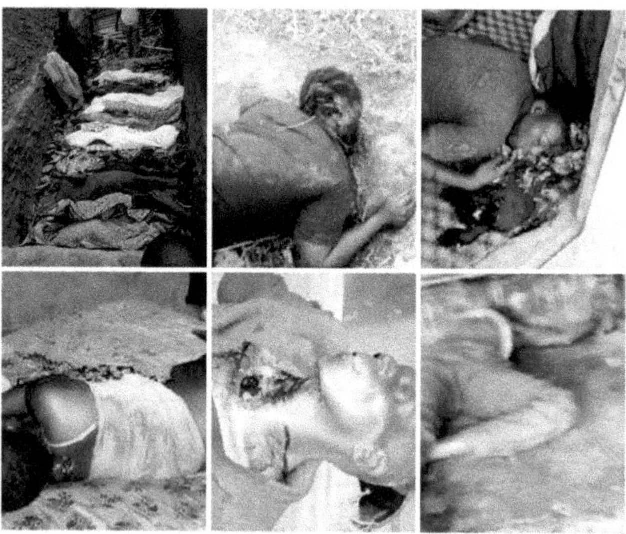

Those injured included Abinso Yusuf, Isaiah Jonathan, Markus Kukuri, Philip Magaji, Magaji Ma'aji, and Zipporah Jonathan.

As could be observed through some of their names, the victims were Christians. They are indigenes of Gonan Rogo. The Fulani people who lived in the community were not affected because, as noted by SOKAPU Nigeria in their statement, "... Fulani and Muslim neighbours, some who have been living around the community for 40 years, had quietly left in the night before the attack[17]." This revelation alleges communication and conspiracy between the Fulani herdsmen and their settled counterparts. It points to the possibility of a hidden agenda calculated to exterminate the Christian ethnic minorities clustering on North-Central Nigeria, forming a barrier against the expansion of Fulani's Sokoto Caliphate, its power, and Islamic influence - which comes beside the quest for greener pastoral terrain down south.

Indeed, attempts by the Fulanis to flush out over thirty ethnic groups that are predominantly Christians in Southern Kaduna has spanned decades. The confrontation usually comes in various shades and forms. For instance, in 1987, there was an outbreak of violence in the College of Education, Kafanchan, where scores of Christians were killed, churches torched, and properties worth millions of naira destroyed due to alleged misinterpretation and interpretation of the Quran. Again in 1992, the indigenous Christians at Zango Kataf were attacked on two occasions by Muslim residents over the dispute stemmed from the relocation of the town's market by the state government against Muslim interest to the outskirts area. The Christians in Southern Kaduna, twice again, became victims of the Sharia crisis of 2001 and the Post-Presidential election crisis of 2011. The perennial conflict later changed its colors and took the form of herdsmen-farmers disputes but with a marked genocidal and jihadist drive. Since May 2016, violent clashes in Southern Kaduna mostly come in the form of Fulani herdsmen attacking Christian farmers. On the attackers' nature, reports obtained from the interviews at Kachia Local Government Council Secretariat by Abdulbarkindo Adamu, Alupsen Ben, and Gloria C (2018) have it that the attackers usually take their Christian targets unawares[18]. The timing of these attacks mostly occur in the night, and in killing their victims, the herdsmen do not even spare the vulnerable such as the aged, women, and children[19].

Showing Fulani's effort at ethnic cleansing, his hatred of indigenous allegiance to the Christian religion through casualty data gathered from three local government areas located in Southern Kaduna. The data reveals that the overall number of indigenous Christians killed between May 2016 and September 2017 is approximately seven hundred and nine (709), while that of Muslims killed by the Christians' reprisal attacks is about sixteen (16)[20] . Data culled from the Africa Conflict and Security Analysis Network (ACSAN) below:

LGA	Christians Killed	Muslims Killed
Jema'a	327	1
Kaura	236	14
Sanga	146	1
Total	**709**	**16**

Source: Africa Conflict and Security Analysis Network (ACSAN), 10th January 2018

The experience of heavy killings of indigenous Christians in the whole of Southern Kaduna is not far from what has been expressed in the table above. A similar situation has also been experienced in Benue State, where indigenous people, predominantly Christians, have been massacred by the rampaging Fulani herdsmen in rapid succession to clear North-Central Nigeria for the entrenchment of the Fulani system.

The Benue State Commissioner for Information and Orientation, Mr. Lawrence Onoja Jnr., while speaking at a press conference at Makurdi, the state capital, released a timeline of Fulani Herdsmen attack Benue State from February 2013 to May 2017 and presented as follows:

1. February 2013: Fulani attacked Agatu burning Inoli, Ologba, Olegeje, Olegogboche, Olegede, Adana, Inminy, and Abugbe communities. Many lives were lost.
2. 23rd April, 2013: 10 farmers were killed in an attack on the Mbasenge community in Guma LGA by suspected herdsmen.
3. 7th May, 2013: 47 mourners gunned down in Agatu while burying two police officers killed the Tuesday before in Nassarawa.
4. 14th May, 2013: Over 200 herdsmen surround Ekwo-Okpanchenyi, Agatu LGA, killing 40 locals.
5. 5th July, 2013: 20 people were killed in a “conflict” between Tiv farmers & herdsmen at Nzorov, Guma LGA, Benue state.
6. 31st July, 2013: Herdsmen invaded two villages in Agatu LGA, killing eight villagers allegedly retaliating

for killing 112 cows.

7. 7th November, 2013: Attackers strike at Ikpele & Okpopolo communities, killing seven and displacing over 6000 inhabitants.
8. 9th November, 2013: 36 locals were killed and seven villages overrun in an attack by herdsmen on Agatu LGA locals.
9. 20th November, 2013: Attack on communities in Guma LGA, killing 22 locals and destroying properties worth millions of naira.
10. 20th January, 2014: Gunmen attacked Agatu LGA, killing five soldiers and seven civilians.
11. 20th January, 2014: Attack on Adeke village. Three dead.
12. February 20-21, 2014: Herdsmen attacked Gwer West LGA. Thirty-five people were killed, eighty thousand displaced, and six Council Wards sacked.
13. 24th February, 2014: Attack on a Tiv community along Naka road, Makurdi, killing eight people.
14. 6th March, 2014: 30 killed in Kwande, Katsina/Ala, and Logo LGAs by attackers dressed in military uniforms. Six villages sacked.
15. 12th March, 2014: Raid on Ukpam village of Mbabaai in Guma LGA. Twenty-eight persons were killed. Yam barns and farms burnt.
16. 10th March, 2014: Herdsmen attacked former Governor Suswam's convoy at Umenger. He and his convoy managed to escape.
17. 12th March, 2014: Herdsmen attack Suswam's village in Logo LGA. 22 slaughtered. The entire village sacked.
18. 23rd March, 2014: 25 killed and over 50 injured by herdsmen said to be bearing sophisticated weapons in

Gbajimba, Guma LGA.

19. 25th March, 2014: Police recovered seven corpses following an attack on Agena village by Herdsmen.
20. 29th March, 2014: Herdsmen attacked four villages in Agatu LGA. Nineteen people were killed, 15 others were abducted.
21. 29th March, 2014: Suspected use of chemical weapons on Shengev community in Gwer West LGA, leaving 15 people dead.
22. 30th March, 2014:19 locals killed and 15 abducted in Agatu LGA.
23. 10th April, 2014: Over 100 herdsmen attacked four villages in Ukemberaga/Tswarev ward of Logo LG, 6 killed, properties lost.
24. 15th April, 2014: Attack on Obagaji, Headquarters of Agatu LGA, 12 youths killed.
25. 10th September, 2014: Herdsmen attacked five villages in Ogbadibo LGA, leaving scores dead.
26. 27th January, 2015: 17 persons killed in Abugbe, Okoklo, Ogwule & Ocholoyan in Agatu LGA by herdsmen.
27. 30th January, 2015: Over 100 attackers stormed five villages in Logo LGA, killing nine persons in the attack.
28. 15th March, 2015: herdsmen sacked Egba village in Agatu LGA; over 90 locals, including women and children, were killed.
29. 27th April, 2015: 28 persons killed by herdsmen in attack on three villages at Mbadwem, Guma LGA; houses and farmlands razed.
30. 11th May, 2015: herdsmen invaded the Ikyoawen community in Turan Kwande LGA. 5 persons were killed and eight others wounded.

31. 24th May, 2015: 100 killed in an attack by herdsmen in villages and refugee camps at Ukura, Gafa, Per, and Tse-Gusa, Logo LGA.
32. 7th July, 2015: 1 local killed and several others injured following an attack on mourners in Imande Bebeshi in Kwande LGA.
33. 5th November, 2015: 12 persons killed, 25 others injured in Buruku LGA following an attack by suspected herdsmen.
34. 8th February, 2016: 10 killed and over 300 displaced in clash between herdsmen and farmers at Tor-Anyiin and Tor-Ataan in Buruku LGA.
35. February 21-24, 2016: Over 500 locals were killed and 7000 displaced in an attack on Agatu LGA by Fulani herdsmen. Over seven villages razed.
36. 9th March, 2016: herdsmen killed eight residents in attacks on Ngorukgan, Tse Chia, Deghkia, and Nhumbe in Logo LGA.
37. 11th March, 2016: Attack on Convoy of Senator David Mark by suspected herdsmen in Agatu LGA. No casualty was recorded.
38. 13th March, 2016: 6 people, including an APC youth leader, were killed by herdsmen in an attack on Tarka LGA.
39. 29th February, 2016: 11 killed in Edugbeho Agatu LG, including a police inspector.
40. 10th March, 2016: Two killed in attack on Obagaji Agatu.
41. 5th March, 2016: Houses burnt in Agatu. Security forces prevented killings.
42. 24th January, 2017: 15 persons were killed by rampaging Fulani herdsmen, who attacked farmers in

Ipiga village in Ohimini Local Government Area of Benue State.

43. 2nd March, 2017: No fewer than ten persons were killed in a renewed hostility between herdsmen and farmers in the Mbahimin community, Gwer East Local Government Area of Benue State.
44. 11th March, 2017: Seven people were killed when herdsmen attacked a Tiv community, Mkgovur village in Buruku local government area of Benue State.
45. 8th May, 2017: Three persons were confirmed killed by herdsmen in Tse-Akaa village, Ugondo Mbamar District of Logo Local Government Area of Benue State.
46. 13th May, 2017: Less than one week after herdsmen killed many people in three communities of Logo Local Government Area of Benue State, armed herders struck again on 13th May, killing eight more people[21].

Another North-Central State that has repeatedly been visited by Fulani herdsmen carnage in Plateau. An ethnic pluralistic state confronted by age-long Muslim-Christian tension, Plateau is known to be the theatre of bloodletting since 2001, when clashes between indigenes and mainly Hausa-Fulani non-indigenes began to assume horrifying dimension. The Fulani herdsmen's killings continue the ethnoreligious crisis, all dressed in a different toga. Of course, the Hausa-Fulani indigenes of Jos Plateau have been claiming that their ancestors were original founders of Jos. This position is seriously contested by their ethnic Afizere, Anaguta, and Berom neighbors[22]. An unnamed eyewitness who spoke with the Sahara Reporters following the killings of about 17 persons.

This includes a pregnant woman killed by Fulani herdsmen in January 2020 in Robi community in Bokkos Local Government Area, said: "There was no disagreement; they wrote on our walls that they are going to drive us away from our land because they said the land belonged to them[23]"

As of 2012, the Fulani herdsmen had already kick-started what would become a recurring tragedy in Plateau State - that is, the jihad against Christianity and genocidal onslaught against other ethnic nationalities in the State. One memorable event was the death of Senator Gyan Dantong and the then-Majority Leader of the Plateau State House of Assembly, Mr. Gyan Fulani. The duo died in a stampede that occurred while attending a mass burial event of about 50 victims massacred by Fulani herdsmen at Maseh village in Riyom Local Government Area. Another such of the intermittent violent clashes in this North-Central State where the Muslim North meets the Christian South occurred in June 2018 with over 86 people losing their lives while about 50 houses were set ablaze[24]. On Monday 27th January 2020, no fewer than 13 persons in Bokkos Local Government Area were confirmed dead in an attack by suspected Fulani gunmen barely two weeks after suspected herdsmen killed 12 people in Mangu Local Government Area of Plateau State[25].

The Fulani herdsmen had spread their tentacles of violence from the Middle-belt of the country to the Southern States. On one occasion, there was an allegation of a helicopter flying over the forest area of Arimogija community in Ose Council Area of Ondo State, a southwestern state, and dropping some ammunition for the herdsmen[26]. In March 2020, Fulani herdsmen reportedly killed a rice farmer, Jacob Odushe, his son, Adura, and another young lad, Victor Ejeh, thus making the residents flee the community. In the Southwest, news of kidnapping by herdsmen are rampant. Back in September 2015, six suspected Fulani herdsmen had kidnapped a prominent Yoruba Christian, Chief Olu Falae - a former Presidential candidate who contested on the joint platform of the Alliance for Democracy (AD) and the All People's Party (APP) against Chief Olusegun Obasanjo of the Peoples Democratic Party (PDP) in 1999; he also served both as Secretary to the military government and as a Minister of Finance during Ibrahim Babangida regime. The abductors seized Chief Falae at his Ilado farm in Akure, the Ondo State capital, and released him following an alleged payment of about 5-million-naira ransom to the kidnappers. In April the following year, about ten herdsmen invaded Falae's farm again, killing one of his Oodua Peoples' Congress, OPC, guards. In May 2019, Prof. Olayinka Adegbehinde, an orthopedic surgeon at the Obafemi Awolowo University, Ile-Ife, Osun State, was reportedly kidnapped by Fulani herdsmen on his way from Lagos. He was eventually released after the payment of about 5-million-naira ransom[27]. The killing of the second child of the Afenifere Chairman, Pa Reuben Fasoranti, Mrs. Funke Olakunrin, by suspected herdsmen in July 2019 sparked the outrage of the Yoruba ethnics and other Nigerians. Their presence in the Southwest elicits fears in the minds of the indigenes. In May 2019, some women in Ondo State staged a demonstration on Akure's streets, through the Deji of Akure's palace, to protest what they described as a takeover of their homeland by herdsmen. They lamented over alleged rape, molestation, and destruction of their farmlands and livestock. They further stressed that they could not travel because of incessant kidnappings by the herdsmen[28].

In the Southeast region, from Enugu to Ebonyi, Anambra to Abia, there have been reports of killings by Fulani herdsmen[29]. One major attack prosecuted by the Fulani herdsmen militants in Igboland took place on Monday, 25th April 2016. According to the Vanguard report, about 40 persons were said to have been slaughtered in Nimbo, Uzo-Uwani Local Government Area of Enugu State by no fewer than 500 heavily-armed herdsmen.[30] About seven villages in Nimbo (Nimbo Ngwoko, Ugwuijoro, Ekwuru, Ebor, Enugu Nimbo, Unuome, and Ugwuachara) were among the areas attacked, and about ten residential homes, including a church, Christ Holy Church International, a.k.a. Odozi Obodo, were reportedly burnt down by the herdsmen[31]. This shows how prepared the Fulani are in taking their mission very far away from their domain in the Northwest of Nigeria.

In the South-South, tension also peaked as the Fulani herdsmen intensified their criminal activities in the region. In Delta State, after the alleged killing of about 14 persons in Avwon, Agadama, and Ohoror communities in Ugheli Local Government Area in February 2020, the State Commissioner for Higher Education, Professor Patrick Muoboghare, narrated to The Guardian newspaper many atrocities the people endured in the hands of the marauding herdsmen. He said: "In the last few years, they had killed not less than 50 people in the community, and now resorted to yearly killings as a plot by the Fulani herdsmen to take over our land. Some Fulani herdsmen were arrested and handed over to the police before now. Still, they were promptly freed because the police national command structure is in the hands of Fulani officers[32]."

One could only imagine how some ragtag nomadic herdsmen

could be so powerful to the extent of holding the country by the jugular. It is not that they suddenly emerge from the blues to unleash brutality on Nigerians, but the fact is that, for ages, they have always been there tending their cattle. Back then, trouble would only occur on a lighter scale whenever their cows damage farmers' crops. This would rage the farmers to retaliate by rustling their cattle. There would be peaceful settlement without any attempt at wiping out the entire community such as we see today. However, the character of the herdsmen-farmers dispute had changed a few years after 2010. *This begs the question; how could ordinary herdsmen afford sophisticated arms and ammunitions capable of taking out a whole community, and where is the central command for such operations?*

You do not need a soothsayer to affirm that the herdsmen militants are under the instructions of powerful Fulani syndicates who own these cattle. These cattle owners are apparently in government, military, politics, business, education, and all fields of human endeavor. Despite their various occupations, these Fulani top shots place a premium on cattle and invest in rearing them. As they invest in cattle, they also dictate their objectives to their employees. They armed the herdsmen to execute their agenda - an agenda necessitated by the challenge of Fulani's (Sokoto Caliphate) Islamic supremacy in the North by Kanuri-led Old Kanem-Bornu Islamic bloc. From 2009, Kanuri began to extend their influence from the Northeast towards North-central Nigeria by way of Boko Haram militancy. The Fulani responded by militarizing pastoralism to insulate Kanuri's Boko Haram offensive tactically. The two militant groups from the rival Islamic blocs wouldn't confront each other; hence they take their aggression on Christian ethnic minorities. While Boko Haram deal decisively with Christian communities in the Northeast, the Fulani take over the middle-belt to expand their sphere of influence towards southern Nigeria. The Fulani had to take their act of evil a notch further when they observed the Nigerian Federal Government was taking Boko Haram more seriously by making concessions to the Kanuris.

The unabated killings by the Fulani herdsmen are beyond the wants of grazing space. According to the Business Day newspaper, some commentators on this matter had pointed to an agenda other than herders-farmers conflicts. While Mr. Yinka Odumakin, a member of the Southern Nigeria Middle Belt Forum, alleged an attempt by Fulani to exterminate different ethnic nationalities to take over their land, Mr. Alfred Okom, a Jos-based businessman, said the killings have a religious tinge. According to Odumakin, "The media must stop this wrong narrative that it is a farmers-herdsmen crisis. There is nothing like that; it is purely Fulani herdsmen killing people. There is a plan to kill people and take over their land."

On the other hand, Okom said: "Look at the pattern, whether it is in Adamawa, Zamfara, Benue, Niger, Taraba or Plateau, the target is the Christian community. Remember, they invaded a Catholic Church in Benue last April (2018) and slaughtered two priests and other parishioners. In Adamawa, they have killed many Christians and burnt churches. They carry out open killings of the Christian faithful in people's full glare, and nobody challenges them. In the latest attack on Plateau State, they killed many people in the church and burnt down many worship centers. *The question is, what has the church got to do with grazing and herdsmen?* Considering they have a plan to convert, by force, everybody to Islam and acquire more territories, they take advantage of a weak government or a government that may be sharing that agenda; otherwise, this shouldn't be happening in any country ruled by human beings[33]."

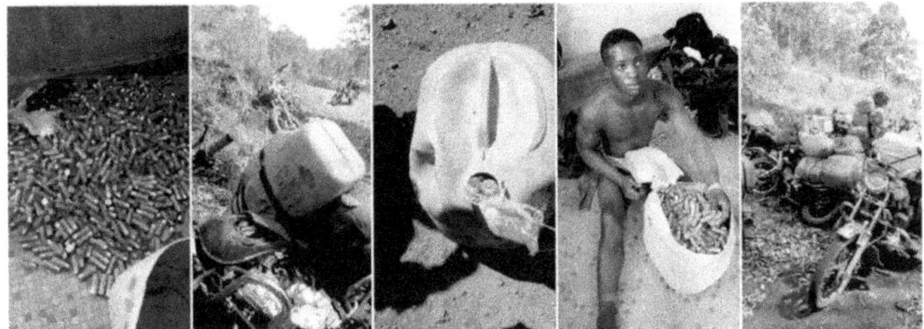

CHAPTER TWO

THE FULANI CODES AND INTEREST IN PASTORALISM, PIETY AND POWER (3Ps)

The fragmentation of African ethnic groups by European powers into various colonies in the 19th and 20th centuries had fundamentally led to the Fulanis forming a part of the population of over 17 countries in post-colonial sub-Saharan Africa. Variously known as Fulani, Fula, Fulbe, or in French-speaking countries as Peul and Hilani. This ethnic group lives in Senegal, Mauritania, Guinea, Mali, Gambia, Nigeria, Benin, Sierra Leone, Burkina Faso, Ivory Coast, Guinea Bissau, Togo, Cameroun, Niger, Liberia, Ghana, and Suda[1]. The Fulani spread through the Sahel grasslands, at the territory from modern Senegal to Sudan[2].

Fulani language is variously known as "Fulfude," "Pulaar," "Fula," or "Peul," among other names. It belongs to the Niger-Congo group's West African sub-family, along with Wolof, Serer, and Temne[3]. There are many variations and dialects of Fulfude, but the influence of surrounding peoples is clearly seen in its local variations[4].

Fulani may be broadly classified into two: The Town Fulani called Toroobe or 'Fulani Gida' (Sedentary Fulani). They have settled in towns and intermarried with the settled farmers such as the Hausa and acquired pure Negroid features[5]. The others, the Cattle or Cow Fulani or 'Bororoje,' live as nomadic cattle-keepers. They are also kept separate from the settled communities and manage their affairs independently of the people they lived with. Because of this independent existence, the Cow Fulani have retained much of their original Fulani features[6].

According to K.B.C. Onwubiko, the Fulani first appeared in West Africa history in Tekrur in about the 9th Century, and this is regarded as their probable place of origin in West Africa. Quoting J.O. Hunwick, "the Fulani trace their origin in West Africa back to Futa Toro in Senegal..."[7] He, therefore, notes that Futa Toro was the successor state of the ancient state of Tekrur[8]. The oral history of the Fulanis also contains information about their migration from Futa Toro and Macina towards the east. By the 15th Century, we can see, from available records, a steady flow of Fulani migration in Hausaland, Bornu, and other regions in northern Nigeria.

Despite the interaction with other people, the Fulani have distinct features that distinguish them from other ethnic groups. Principal amongst these is the ancestral concept of pulaaku that accords the Fulani an identity. The word pulaaku serves as an unwritten code of conduct for the Fulani people[9]. It has no clear-cut translation in the English language, but it holds identity, pride, and value in their hearts to the Fulani. Pulaaku could, at best, be described as an abstraction that hinges on the Fulfude words pullo (referring to Fulani) and Pulaade (meaning to act like Fulani)[10]. In the word pulaaku, items are often seen in some writings, as rightly noted by Marquerite Dupire, as consisting of deeply rooted personality traits that distinguish the Fulani. From other ethnic groups, moral standards and social codes that guide an individual's conduct towards others and establish critical social institutions and patterns of behavior through which Fulani express and signal ethnic identity with each other and separation from others[11].

According to a popular submission attempting to sum up the Fulani codes, pulaaku "portrays the ideal Fulani as one who has stoic sobriety, reserve and strong emotional ties to cattle. At the same time, the model Fulani is gentle in demeanor. His carriage conveys a proud reserve, almost a disdain toward non-Fulani. It is said that no one knows what a Fulani is thinking. The real Fulani is physically, as well as psychologically distant from other people, especially non-Fulani.

Moreover, he is enjoined from displays of strong emotions. His demeanor is taciturn, loathing the boisterousness of others. Wealth is not to be vulgarly displayed but carefully and quietly tended[12]."

As pointed out by Schareika (2010), "pulaaku notion was used to unite a group by praising the common values of pulaaku as the decisive group trait and pointing, in moral indignation, to excluded groups that purportedly do not stick to these values[13]." In a way, Fulani's pulaaku is akin to Zeno's stoicism. Zeno (a Hellenistic philosopher who lived between 334-262 B.C.E) preached that "Man conquers the world by conquering himself[14]." He harped on the value of "apatheia" (or absence of pleasure), which holds that by controlling one's emotions and physical desires one could develop wisdom and know-how to apply it. For a man to accept his fate, according to Zeno, is nothing more than the belief: what happens, happens, and there is no point complaining about it[15]. Sparta probably inspired this philosophy in ancient Greece. Sparta was a city-state known for its powerful army and incredible feats during the Peloponnesian War (431-404 BCE).

The Fulani codes could be seen as aspects of Spartans' stoic concept, which hinges mainly on self-discipline, courage, and code of honor. Stoicism has to do with tolerating tough situations without expressing feelings. Like the Spartans, a

Fulani observing pulaaku is known to speak sparingly to others, and no one knows what he thinks as he is often seen withdrawn. As enigmatic as the Spartans, the Fulanis could be unpredictable. They cultivate the external appearance that reflects their internal prowess. Fulanis, like Spartans, value simplicity, austerity, and frugality, and all these make them be at comfort with discomfort[16].

In terms of courage, the Ngorgu concept in Fulani's pulaaku encourages them to stand tall and confront their challenge fearlessly. Like Spartans, cardinal virtues of self-discipline and courage make them renowned and feared for their military might. The Fulani herdsmen militants might have acted as Spartans by showing self-mastery and courage in prosecuting the jihad cum genocide against rival religious and ethnic groups. Since the Fulani militants endure the extremities of climate and weather conditions, they can cover distances notwithstanding; endure hunger, and stay on wait overnight for their targets. They find convenience in the discomfort of bushes, forests, and arid terrains. Men that are not given to luxuries can hardly feel inconvenience in a primeval way of life; whether they find themselves in the coldest of nights or under scotching sun, their mission is always unflinching. They are able to capture their targets deep in their slumber, perhaps in the warmth of their spouses when they are very weak and cannot pull themselves together to defend their lives nor fight the horror of the midnight goons. The well-armed Fulani militants know how to visit their targets in the dark, cold hours when they are unprepared, slitting their throats or smashing them to death.

Fulanis should not be seen as sociopaths or as a feral race that solely embarks on killings. They could be very accommodating and hospitable too. They wouldn't just kill without a set agenda. However, it seems they have been able to weave a particular interest around their agenda, which combines the "3Ps" of Pastoralism, Piety, and Power. Their pulaaku codes stress the symbolic importance of cattle rearing in defining the Fulani ethnicity. The codes also cognize the use of Islam as a means of distinguishing Fulani from others[17]. Nonetheless, the Fulanis might not actualize their agenda in a pugnaciously competitive, pluralistic country as Nigeria without a firm hold on political power.

Fulani Interest in Pastoralism

In the account of K.B.C. Onwubiko, the Fulani were at first wholly pastoralists. After the fall of Old Ghana in the 13th Century, they started spreading eastwards[18]. Some later abandoned their traditional nomadic way of life and settled in towns[19]. Notwithstanding, the Fulani today is forming the largest pastoral nomadic group in the world[20]. Cattle remain a significant symbolic repository of their values[21]. Their pulaaku code also helps in stressing the symbolic importance of cattle in defining Fulani ethnicity[22]. Elizabeth Soriola brings appropriate Fula sayings to the fore in order to underscore the importance of cattle to Fulani's existence. The proverb says: "Cattle surpass everything," "it's even more important than father and mother," "if cattle die, then Fulbe dies[23]."

Interestingly, these sayings show how cattle occupy the importance of place in Fula culture and traditions. Some Fulani wouldn't mind placing the value of cattle over human life.

In fact, there was a mild drama in the Nigerian Federal House of Representatives when a female lawmaker, Aishatu Dukku, representing Dukku/Nafada Federal Constituency in Gombe State, made a statement during a plenary session on Wednesday 17th January 2018, when the house was discussing Fulani massacres in Benue and Taraba States. She said: "Yes, the herdsman values even the life of the cow more than his own life; that is how God created him[24]." Although she was immediately rebuked by her colleague, Mr. Hassan Saleh, a representative of Ado/Obadigbo/Opkokwu Federal Constituency in Benue State, who said, "No cow, not even 10 billion cows has enough value like a human being[25]." Albeit, Dikku was supported by the Miyetti Allah Chairman in the North-East, Alhaji Mafindi Danburam. He reechoed that it is true that God created a Fulani man to value a cow's life more than human life[26].

The pastoral Fulani are almost exclusively cattlemen, and their herds are based on their social and economic life[27]. Recall that 56 year-Fulani herdsmen, Mohammed Abdulkadire, jumped into River Benue in Logo Local Government Area as reported by the Sunday Punch newspaper to take his life over his cows' death[28]. As narrated by Benue State Chapter National Coordinator of Miyetti Allah Cattle Breeders Association of Nigeria, Garus Gololo, the deceased committed suicide after losing 200 of his own cows to hunger and lack of water[29]. This confirmed that the socio-economic life of a Fulani herder revolved around their cattle. If they could value cows more than human life, it is possible to kill humans found to be problematic to the cattle's survival.

The Fulani's absolute interest in the cattle enterprise is fetching them socio-economic rewards, but it has also, most importantly, borne them a very impressive cultural ideal of courage. As noted by Professors Dale Lott and Benjamin Hart, their culture has made a general social virtue of the personality trait of aggressive dominance that is vital in the husbandry of the cattle[30]. These scholars observe that a herdsman is unquestionably dominant over all his cattle. One feature of the husbandry that illustrates this is the fine degree of control he has over the herd's movement. At the same time, grazing - no halters, ropes, or restraint devices are used[31].

Pointing to the probable force behind the maintenance of domination over cattle by the Fulani, Lott, and Hart (1977) asserted that such is illustrated by Fulani's response to 'broadside' threats by herd bulls[32]. According to them, it would seem possible that the Fulanis would develop specific behavior toward their cattle that is not generalized to their human social relationships, the procedures involved in the training of the boys to be aggressive towards the bulls. Their failure to make bulls subordinate is not criticized as poor animal husbandry but as cowardice[33].

Lott et al. (1977) revealed in their study that when Fulanis were asked what distinguished them from other people, their answers emphasized a single characteristic - courage, both in the sense of lacking fear and being able to overcome it. They said this high level of courage explained their ability to handle cattle, an ability in which they admit to peers. They asserted that cattle were dangerous and that everyone except Fulanis was afraid of them[34].

In creating an argument that the need to be aggressive in

dominating the cattle might influence the assertive character of a herder, Ekvall (1964) purported that it was the special demands on nomadic people for an assertive, decisive lifestyle and ability to respond to threats to their animals from weather or predators[35]. And the way pastoralism influenced the cultural ideal of the Fulani has led Johnson (1967) to believe that their quest for political domination is "presumably facilitated by an aggressive personality[36]."

Fulani And Piety

The Fulani are known for Islamic piety. Islamism forms the core of their culture and worldview. They systematically use Islam to distinguish themselves from others and as a veritable tool for converting other ethnic nationalities to the Fulani system. It could therefore be said that conversion to Islam is synonymous with Fulanization. This is called an ethnic conversion. For instance, in the Middle Belt of Nigeria, where the Islamic North meets indigenous ethnic Christians, there are serious Fulani attempts at ethnic conversion. Johannes (2006), while noting that ownership of land at the Middle Belt is contested between Hausa/Fulani "settlers" from the North and the "indigenous" ethnic groups which are mostly Christians and traditionalists, avows that the migrants who are still a minority, try to spread their faith among the "native" population[37]. By so doing, "those who convert tend to assume the language, culture, and political loyalties of Hausa-Fulani settlers[38]." Harnischfeger (2006) further illustrated that, with the call to fight for sharia, indigenous Muslims are put under pressure to prove that their new faith was more important to them than their old ethnic loyalties[39]. When armed conflicts broke out, most converts sided with the Hausa-Fulani migrants and fought against their (former) Christian or traditional kin in the name of religion[40].

In African societies, religion tends to be the life-blood of morality and a root from which societal set of beliefs or worldview spring. Therefore, according to Ron Hubbard, the most critical point of attack on culture becomes its religious experience[41]. According to him, "where one can destroy or undermine religious institutions, then the entire fabric of the society can be quickly subverted or brought to ruin[42]." The Fulanis seem to understand this religious strategy perfectly well as they use Islamic identity to garner support from Fulanized populations in pursuit of their agenda.

Herdsmen atrocities in Nigeria should be seen in the context of Uthman Dan Fodio's war of jihad: "*Allah prescribed the jihad upon us in order to remove us from the harm which arises from leaning towards an impure world and clinging to its things which actually amount to nothing and the only benefit from it is regret*[43]." Using herdsmen to prosecute an Islamic agenda in Nigeria is a cue taken from radical Islamism in pre-colonial Africa, which was mainly originated in nomadic revivalist movements. The role of nomads in Islamic jihad in Africa could be traced back to the time that Arab Islamic forces defeated the Byzantine army in the middle of the 7th Century and gained control over coastal North Africa, converting the nomad Berber tribes to Islam[44]. It was these Berber speaking nomads who helped to spread Islam in the region between Maghreb (North Africa) and Western Sudan (known to Arabs as Bilad-al Sudan or "Land of the Black")[45]. The spread of Islam has since been reinforced both by the migration of other nomads from across the Sahel over the centuries and the rise of contemporary terrorist organizations[46]. There has been a resurgence of violent conflict and Islamic jihad perpetrated by Muslim nomads belonging to the Hausa-Fulani group in Nigeria[47].

The wanton violence unleashed by Muslim herdsmen on indigenous Christians in Nigeria is perpetrated out of Islamic expansionist tendencies. As referenced in a report, a Hausa-Fulani Muslim nomad is said to have argued: "Komai na Allah ne. Ko wane fili na Allah ne, ba naku ba, ba na kafirai ba, na Allah ne"[48]. (Translation: Everything belongs to Allah. Every piece of land belongs to Allah and not you; it is not for you infidels but for Allah). According to Abdulbarkindo Adamu et al (2018), the sovereignty of Allah is understood as being the foundation for all socio-political and economic systems. Hence, society must be governed in accordance with the Quran and Sunna[49]. This means that human beings must, individually and collectively, surrender all lordship rights, legislation, and authority over others. No person, class, or group can lay claim to sovereignty. Allah is the real lawgiver, and absolute legislation rests in him.

Consequently, when a Hausa-Fulani Muslim herdsman claims that every piece of land belongs to Allah, it means the land belongs to the Muslim-God and by a right to the Muslims. The Hausa-Fulani Muslim herdsman, therefore, understands that he has a right not only to the land but a religious obligation to ensure that Islam reigns supreme over that land[50]. This understanding of Allah is based on the distinction between darul Islam, the house of Islam, and darul al-harb, the house of war. The former is composed of the Muslim faithful, while the latter refers to those within the realm of the infidels[51]. Over time, jihad has come to mean the struggle against the devil or one's own desires (nafs), as well as fighting those of non-Islamic faith[52]. This includes waging war against unbelievers to convert them to Islam and encourages a biased outlook and the view that conquering non-Muslim territories for Allah is a religious duty[53].

Fulani and Quest for Power

On Saturday, 6th June 2020, the Nigerian media space was heated by an interview granted by the National President of Miyetti Allah Kautal Hore, Alhaji Bello Abdullahi Bodejo, to Mr. Vincent Kalu of The Sun newspaper. The leader of the Fulani socio-cultural group said:

> *I don't see any place where people will try and drive away from the Fulani; they have a right in this country. They produced Nigeria. They produced the first Prime Minister. If they produced the first president, another president, another president, and so on, are they not the country's owner? Fulanis are ruling Nigeria, and they must continue to lead the country forever. That is the truth*[54].

Of course, Abdullahi Badejo was aptly reechoing the declaration of late Premier of defunct Northern Nigeria, Alhaji Ahmadu Bello, who was at the time, the prime-mover of Fulani power agenda in the post-independent Nigeria. The country was exactly 12 days after attaining sovereign statehood when Bello's interview announcing Fula power ambition was published in the Parrot Newspaper edition of 12th October 1960 as recollected by *Don Ubani of This Day Live*[55]. It is on record that the Sardauna of Sokoto granted an interview to a foreign journalist during which he said that:

> *"The newly independent nation called Nigeria should be an estate of our great grandfather, Uthman dan Fodio. We must ruthlessly prevent a change of power. we must use the minorities of the North as willing tools and the South as conquered territory and never allow them to rule over their future*[56]*."*

Back in 1957, the same Alhaji Ahmadu Bello, a member of the Sokoto Caliphate Dynasty, was said to have been boasting that the North would continue to conquer the South after the British would have left and that he would personally dip the Quran into the Atlantic Ocean[57].

The quest for power domination by the Fulani in Nigeria could be understood through psycho-religious and historical contexts. First, the Uthman dan Fodio's jihad in the 19th Century was Fulani's revolt against their being political subjects to various Hausa city-states' impious leaderships. They considered themselves more superior to be controlled by the unserious Habe Muslims and pagans. This superiority mindset runs through generations with the consciousness that Fulanizing other groups through Islamization would give Sokoto Caliphate leverage on the power-game. In the Islamic-political formation, the Fulani controls the Caliphate and the Emirates; therefore, becoming a Muslim means the same way of accepting a religiopolitical system that the Fulani take control of. The Fulanis know that they would continue to expand their power base by converting other ethnicities and taking control of them by religious means. For instance, in the event of an election, it is easy for the Fulani to appeal to Muslim populations to vote for a Muslim candidate who might be a Fulani. We could recall how General Muhammadu Buhari (Rtd), in 2001, reportedly called on Muslims to vote for

Muslims in the next presidential election. This shows that the Fulani know how important a Muslim population is to their power agenda; hence, the quest for continuous Islamization by crusade or coercion.

Secondly, the immediate rivals to the Fulani hegemony in the Northern religiopolitical structure are the Kanuris of the Northeast, that is, the region of the Old Kanem-Bornu empire. Perhaps the sudden surge in the Fulani-herdsmen killings wouldn't have been possible in the 2010's if the Fulanis did not sense a Kanuri version of jihad spearheaded by Boko Haram to gain more grounds in the Northern system. Since the enthronement of Sokoto Caliphate in Northern Nigeria by Fulani led dan Fodio and his son, Mohammed Bello, in the first quarter of the 19th Century following the jihad, the Fulanis have been one ethnic entity that stays on top of the Islamic religious and socio-political ladder in the North. In contrast, the Kanuri-led Old Kanem-Bornu bloc in the Northeast plays second fiddle even though the Kanuris of Kanem-Bornu empire led by Muhammed Al-Kanemi were able to resist Fulani jihadists' offensive – an event that ended up in the production of two Islamic power blocs in the North. Sokoto Caliphate is spanning the Northwest to the North-central where Christians, ethnic minorities form barriers, and Old Kanem-Bornu Empire in the Northeast championed by the Kanuri. Therefore, the very act of insulating the expansionist drive of the Sokoto Caliphate by Al-Kanemi's Bornu was not only fueling hostility between the two Islamic powers but plunging them into stiff struggles for religious, cultural, socio-political, and ideological supremacy in which the Fulani still manage to have an edge. Words from the streets of Nigeria has it that the Kanuris, fighting an ethnic course through Boko Haram militancy, have managed to regain lost grounds in the political equation of the northern system and the national front as the Nigerian leadership adopts appeasement approaches to minimize the aggression of Boko Haram militants by way of placing Kanuri elements in the strategic defense positions. Therefore, the probable Fulani suspects that the current Nigerian leadership, with ties to Kanuri ethnicity, is shifting power to the rival Kanuri's northeast Islamic bloc, which may bring the two sections on an equal pedestal - some suspicion that is causing a violent revolt in the guise of herdsmen attacks on Christian, non-Fulani farming communities in the North-central and the southern parts of the country.

The Fulani's pulaaku code has cultivated and nurtured the 3Ps of pastoralism, piety, and power agenda that now places the Fulanis in the strategic and advantageous position to compete in a pluralistic country Nigeria. Their confidence and courage inspired by the code are keys to their mission to convert other ethnicities into their ranks and file as they seek to exert hegemonic control over the whole of Nigeria. Therefore, by the time the entire Nigeria becomes Islamized, the entire country becomes a Fulani property just like the Hausa City States became Fulanized after Uthman dan Fodio's jihad.

CHAPTER THREE

FULANI-HAUSA ALLIANCE, RIVALRY WITH KANURIS AND THE CHALLENGE OF OTHER ETHNIC MINORITIES

First - there is no Hausa race or nation. The word, Hausa, refers more to the language than to the people[1]. Charles Orr (1908) notes:

> *A native will claim to be a Hausa merely because he speaks "the language," and it is not uncommon for pagans and even Fulani to describe themselves as "Hausawa," only because they speak that language. In Hausaland proper, the real Hausa, as distinguished from Fulanis, pagans, Bornuese, & c... is, as it is well known, "Habe"; and this is unquestionably the correct title for the race. In inquiring about ancient rights and customs, one always refers to the "Old Habé Kingdoms" to distinguish what is more loosely called the Hausa States[2].*

Secondly, in making the description more vivid, Onwubiko (1967) presents an old geographical picture of Hausa thus:

> *Between the Kanuri in the east and the Songhai in the west, and stretching from the Niger-Benue junction to the desert south of Agades lies the home of Hausa speaking peoples because the Hausa are not of one tribe or race. They originated from the mingling of different tribes and racial groups of Negro (sic) farmers and nomadic Berbers from the desert. These people have been moulded into something like a nation by the possession of a common language and a common culture[3].*

Thirdly, Abdullahi Sule-Kano of the Department of Political Science at the Usman Dan Fodio University, Sokoto, explains that the historical emergence of the Hausa social formation and the polity were not based on ethnic lines[4]. Drawing attention to Hausa's modern-day cities, he maintains that one "can still find historical imprints that show ethnic identities were not part of the problems of the social relations to the production of African people living in this part of the worl[5]." Sule-Kano would further point out historical imprints of some quarters in Kano and Sokoto - Hausa cities, which were initially occupied by various ethnic nationalities, that have become part and parcel of the cities' identity. On the origin of Kano, he says: "this is the history of the Indabawa, Ayagi, and Yola, quarters of the old Kano City. These were original settlements of the Nupe, Yoruba, and Fulani, respectively[6]. On ancient Sokoto city, Sule-Kano would identify Tadun Nupawa, Wangarawa, and Gobirawa quarters as being the original quarters of the Nupe, the Wangara people (Dyula) from Old Mali, now in the hinterland of Sierra Leone inhabited by the Mandigo and the Gobir people from Gobir who were and are still seen as Sokoto people[7].

As indicated in the previous Chapter, the Fulani had migrated since the 15th Century from the Futa Toro axis in Senegal to the Hausa land, Bornu, including other areas of the Northern half of Nigeria. They specifically settled in towns and villages of Northwestern Hausa land[8], and their settlement produced a high degree of a cultural mix among the indigenes and the "alien" group[9]. The Hausa were mostly pagans, while the Fulani were predominantly Muslims[10]. Adeleye (1971) points out that through the ensuing admixture between the Islamic culture and the indigenous Hausa 'pagan' culture, a gradual polarization of society along the lines of two conflicting religiopolitical ideologies began[11].

As Adeleye (1971) further observed, the Fulani had remained aliens in Hausa and Bornu even though they had lived there for centuries. Without any regard to the substantial number of the learned men among the Fulani, they suffered the disabilities of second-rate citizens among the Hausa[12]. They had no voice in selecting rulers, even as some of the Fulani served in many states' Government at a very high position[13]. The most significant outcome of Fulani isolation, as notes by Adeleye (1971), was a common bond of "Pan-Fulanism[14]." Seclusion seemed to solidify their bond of unity and cohesion among them with "scattered groups in different localities in Hausa land and Borno, nursing deep feelings and resentment against existing governments[15]."

Coupled with Fulani's resentment at their lack of political power, Aremu (2011), a scholar, explained that the declaration of the Jihad of 1804 by Uthman dan Fodio also had more to do with socio-economic problems that were prevalent in Hausa land prior to the jihad[16]. In the same vein, another scholar Crowder (1978), suggested that jihad was a revolt against the illegal and excessive taxation imposed on the masses by the Habe States government, which was widely criticized by Uthman dan Fodio[17]. As reports by Aremu (2011) outlined, "some of the erratic taxes were cattle tax (jingali), market tax, rent for the use of grazing land imposed on the Fulani and the collection of increased tributes from farmers. These illegal extortions, especially the cattle tax, were vehemently opposed and criticized by the Fulani pastoralists[18]." Besides, allegations of corruption were rife against the Government of Habe states. Bribes were given and taken by the officials. Given this untold hardship and cruelty meted on the people and the ostentatious way in which most of the chieftains of Gobir lived, jihad almost became a class struggle between the Hausa-Fulani commoners and their Habe rulers[19].

The whole narrative of Fulani jihad revolves around the life and teachings of Shehu Uthman dan Fodio who was believed to have been born in 1754[20] in Marata, Gobir, to the Toronkawa of Fulani descent[21]. He was also reported to have embarked on missionary journeys to Kebbi, Zamfara, and Gobir where he explained the tenets of Islam, coupled with the use of poems and pamphlets written in Arabic, Fulfude, and Hausa languages. As a reward, he won many admirers and followers across the whole of Hausa land[22]. As emphasized by Aremu (2011), "by the turn of the 19th Century, the Shehu's power had grown considerably that, he had groups of supporters scattered throughout Gobir, Zamfara, and Kebbi who were willing to come to his support in trying times. It was this widespread allegiance to him and his ideals which were to be crucial when the final clash with authority came in 1804[23]."

Judging from the situation highlighted above, Aremu (2011) further observed that the jihadists needed only a little awakening to take up arms in the eventual outbreak of war as they were already indoctrinated for such an action[24]. As noted earlier, Uthman dan Fodio had gained massive popularity and teeming followership; unfortunately, this was to attract the wrath of the rulers of Gobir[25]. Beginning from Bawa in 1789 - 1790 to Yunfa in 1801, the Kings of Gobir attempted, through series of legislation, to restrict Uthman dan Fodio's power and authority to preach and to curtail the activities of his Juma'a[26]. In a way, this culminated in Yunfa's attack on Abd al-Salam, a staunch disciple of Uthman dan Fodio who lived at Gimbassa[27]. The stage was now set for the armed confrontation between the jihadists and the Gobir authority.

It would be recalled that Yunfa was one of Uthman dan

Fodio's pupils. In 1802 he succeeded to the throne of Gobir, and he was all out to counter the influence of his former teacher. In the account of Onwubiko (1967), dan Fodio left the (Royal) court and retired to Degel from where he reinforced his verbal attacks on harsh Hausa rule. Yunfa sought to destroy Degel and to kill him and his followers[28]. However, on February 21, 1804, Uthman and his disciples emigrated from Degel in Gobir to Gudu, an incident known as Hajira, which marked the prelude to the declaration of war against the unbelievers.

At Gudu, the Fulani supporters gathered around Uthman dan Fodio, as well as a vast number of Hausa 'talakawa' or common Hausa folks who felt the scotch of oppressive regimes, and he was declared Sarkin Muslimi or Faithful Commander, and thus contributed to the Fulani revolt in Gobir in 1804[29].

But Aremu has noted that the Fulani's resentment at their total lack of political power had induced the view that the jihad was more of a desire to express Fulani nationalism than a religious confrontation[30]. Onwubiko advanced that:

> *Therefore, the jihad was a total war in which the Fulani leaders aimed to seize power and introduce a government favourable to their tribe (sic). This is borne by the fact that the cattle Fulani in Hausa land were mostly pagans rallied in support of Usman dan Fodio out of tribal (sic) loyalty and not Islamic zeal*[31].

Even the Fulani herdsmen had left their cattle to fight on the side of their kin. The herdsmen were reported to have been a reservoir of the workforce for the jihad's military service[32]. Milsome (1979) wrote that herdsmen, "having being accustomed to a hard nomadic life with a long experience of fighting either in self-defense or in the service of others, and given their skilled use of bow and arrow, the Fulani pastoralists proved to be a useful addition to Usman's army[33]."

The Uthman dan Fodio's jihad, which started in 1804 and formally ended in 1810, first succeeded in Gobir. It further succeeded in the old Habe States of Katsina, Daura, Kano, and Zaria. Although it failed in Borno, as we will find out, three emirates of Borno, namely, Gombe, Hadejia, and Katagum, were established notwithstanding. The establishment of new emirates continued till 1859[34].

In the account of Johnson Aremu, "the greatest impact of the jihad was the creation of the vast religiopolitical edifice known as Sokoto Caliphate[35]. Hill (2009) pointed out that: "with the help of a large Fulani cavalry and Hausa peasants, Uthman dan Fodio overthrew the region's Hausa rulers and replaced them with Fulani emirs[36]." The Caliphate was then headed by a caliph but subdivided into Emirates ruled by the Emirs. The consequence of this development is found today as the Fulani still dominate Nigerian politics[37].

Considering the obvious effect of Uthman dan Fodio's jihad, it considerably led to the emergence of the Hausa-Fulani ethnic group[38]. Usman (1979) maintained that "due to long periods of co-existence between Hausa and Fulani, the ethnic line between them had remarkably been blurred[39]." Aremu (2011) added that a common religion and culture enhance this newfound solidarity and that the two groups have since been collaborating in the political dynamics of Nigeria, thus presenting a more "united" North as against the seemingly divided South[40].

The jihad firmly established the Hausa language as a lingua franca of the North. Explaining further, Ikime (1985) remarked that, with the Hausa language's triumph over Fulfude, the Hausa language became the everyday language of the Caliphate, though Arabic remained the language of Islam. The British recognized this lingua franca over a large area of northern Nigeria and used it as the official language of native administration. This promoted the unity of the North[41].

Therefore, the Hausa-Fulani alliance that had emerged after the jihad was not more or less than ethnic conversion. Although the Hausa language survived, the distinct ethnicities that were bonded together by the language fell under the Fulani political domination. Put differently, and the population became Fulani's. Fage (1988) estimated that the newly formed Caliphate covered over 180 000 square miles and had a population of about 10 million people[42]. The jihad was precipitated more by political exclusion and mass economic asphyxiation than religious consideration. Therefore, the new rulers were welcomed as the common people's redeemers from the bondage of the Habe overlords. This support gave impetus to Fulani's ambition to further expand their empire eastwards and southwards.

On the east of the Fulani's Sokoto Caliphate lies a vast territory of the Kanuris. They had already started a building process of the Kanem-Bornu empire believed to have been one of the oldest in the world. Although the Kanuri are the predominant population in the Northeast, there are enclaves of other ethnic minorities. The Kanuri presence in northern Nigeria preceded for centuries the Fulani's migration into the region. They established the Safewa dynasty that lasted for about a millennium. Although various authors reel out conflicting dates at the start of the dynasty, the time would not be later than 774 AD based on numerous available records. The dynasty ended in 1846, and Shehu's (Sheikh) dynasty took over, and it is still running to this day. Dugu, the first known Mai (King), who reportedly ruled the early settlers, established the center of power at N'jimi, situated in the Northeast of the lake. It is worthy of note that the Kanuri's Kanem-Bornu empire had existed in two parts, separated by Lake Chad. Kanem was found down East while Bornu on the West. Kanem existed as the nerve center of political and governmental activities until the 15th Century when the seat of power was moved to Bornu.

Kanuris were the earliest ethnic group in Northern Nigeria that officially embraced Islam. There was considerable contact between Kanem and North Africa. In the 11th Century, about 1090, Mai Umme Jilmi (1085 - 1097) was converted to Islam. With the acceptance of Islam, Kanem became an influential Muslim state in Central Sudan[43].

It was Mai Dunama I who began to undertake territorial expansion and continued steadily until he died in 1150. His successor, Dunama II, assumed the leadership of the empire and continued the territorial expansion agenda. With a formidable cavalry of 30,000 men, Mai Dunama II extended the empire to Fezzan in the North, Adamawa in the South, Bornu, and Kano in the West, and Wadai in the East. The importance of this expansion was that it helped to spread Islam[44].

Following the collapse of the first Kanem-Bornu empire in 1470, which was possible because of internal conflicts, the second Kanem-Bornu empire took off immediately when Mai Ali Ghaji restored order. Mai Ghaji founded the second empire at Bornu with the seat of power at Ngazargamu. He enforced strict adherence to Islamic practices such as Quran studies and the marrying of only four wives. The Mai raised a strong royal army with which he maintained internal peace and extended the kingdom's sway. In the east, he fought the Bulala to a standstill; in the west, he reduced some Hausa States, including Kano, to tribute-paying states; in the North, he extended the kingdom to Borku and Tibesti, and in the South, he halted a Kwararafa invasion of his state[45].

Therefore, when Uthman dan Fodio led a Hausa-Fulani troop on a jihadist mission to Bornu in 1808, it became an entirely difficult experience for his expedition. Although he managed to snatch Gombe, Hadejia, and Katagum from Bornu and capture the capital, Ngazargamu, it was recaptured by a Kanuri army commander and scholar three times, Muhammed al-Kanemi each time. So, Bornu was not brought into direct military submission to Sokoto[46]." Al-Kanemi accused the Fulani of seizing power in Hausaland in the guise of religious revolt[47]. Commenting on Muhammed al-Kanemi's confrontation with Hausa/Fulani, Aisha Umar Yusuf, in her article in Daily Trust, writes thus:

> *Al-Kanemi waged his war against Sokoto with weapons and letters as he desired to thwart dan Fodio's jihad with the same ideological weapons. He carried on a series of theological, legal, and political debates through letters with the Sultan of Sokoto, Uthman dan Fodio, and later with his son, Muhammed Bello. As Sokoto's expansion was predicated upon struggle against paganism, apostasy, and misrule, Al-Kanemi challenged the rights of his neighbors to strike at a state that had been Muslim for at least 800 years*[48].

This would mark the turning point in the Hausa/Fulani-Kanuri relations. In the 1820s, al-Kanemi drove the Fulani out of Bornu, challenging the Sokoto Caliphate, while occupying the Deya-Damaturu area. This was followed by the occupation of the Kotoko City-States of Kusseri, Ngulfai, and Logone after defeating the Bagirmi in 1824[49]. As narrated by Aisha Yusuf, Mai Dunama IX rewarded al-Kanemi with control over a Bornu province on the west. Al-Kanemi strategically assumed the title, Shehu or Sheikh of Bornu[50], thus paving the way for his son, following his death in 1835, to succeed him and seized the empire in 1846. This brought to an end a thousand years of the Sefawa dynasty.

Indeed, the act of halting the expansionist mission of the Sokoto Caliphate by al-Kanemi's Bornu empire was not only bringing hostility between the two Islamic powers but threw them into further rivalry in the areas of ideologies and Islamic literature.

Fulani's Sokoto Caliphate, which thrived on Hausaland, although abolished by the British, existed side-by-side with the former Bornu empire's territory, which is now under the Sheikh or Shehu religious and traditional authority in Northern Nigeria. As it is, the region of the Old Bornu empire is not taking directives from the Sultan of Sokoto when it comes to religious, socio-cultural, and traditional concerns.

Although the British colonialists abolished the political authority of the Sokoto Caliphate after they subdued the Hausa-Fulani forces in the battle of Burmi in 1903, the title of Sultan was spared, and it is still an important religious office for most northern Muslims till the time of this writing. Also, the colonial masters had absorbed the declining Bornu empire along with the Sokoto Caliphate into a single geopolitical area, then known as the Northern Protectorate of Nigeria, before the 1914 amalgamation with the Southern Protectorate.

The threat was the Fulani's expansionist push, originating from the Kanuri to the east and South, emerging from the middle-belt ethnic minorities, riding on the back of European imperialism.

The area called the middle-belt or North-central Nigeria connotes the axis situated along the margin dividing northern from southern Nigeria. Globalsecurity.org describes it as an east-west belt of people and languages, running from the Cameroon Highlands on the east to the Niger River valley on the west and contains 50 to 100 separate languages and ethnic groups. In which varied from the Nupe and Tiv, comprising more than half a million each, to a few hundred speakers of a distinct language in small highland valleys in the Jos Plateau[51]. The area consists of the present-day Adamawa, Taraba, Niger, Kogi, Plateau, Bauchi, Nasarawa, Benue, Kwara, and the Federal Capital Territory.

The major ethnic nations that established powerful kingdoms in the middle-belt were Jukun and Nupe, amongst others. The Jukun founded their kingdom around the Gongola-Benue basin[52]. They formed a powerful pagan kingdom in the 16th Century and threatened the independence of Islamic Hausa and Bornu states. By 1800, the Jukun was paying an annual tribute of 1,000 slaves to Bornu. From being a vassal state to Bornu, it was absorbed into Muri's Fulani emirate and disappeared from history as an independent state.

On the other hand, the Nupe Kingdom, which occupied the low basin between Niger and Kaduna rivers, declined following the disputes over the succession resulted in the splitting of the kingdom under two rival Etsus (kings): Jimada (1796-1805) with his headquarters at Jimi (Gbara) and Mujaja II (1796-1810) with his headquarters at Raba[53]. In 1810, during the Fulani jihad, a Fulani itinerant preacher Mallam Dendo came to Nupe and soon gathered round himself ardent Fulani and Hausa Muslims; while taking advantage of the disputed succession in the Nupe Kingdom. He seized power and became ruler of much of Nupeland but allowed the rival Etsus to reign as puppets[54]. After Dendo died in 1831, the rival Etsus were humbled by a successor called Usman Zaki, who became the first Fulani Etsu of Nupe and ruled Nupeland from Bida[55]. In 1860, Massaba was the king of Nupeland, and he received Dr. William Balfour Baikie during his visit to Bida[56].

Baikie's visit also constituted significant arguments that would change the course of Fulani's expansionist history. There were waves of exploration up River Niger in the mid-19th Century. First of all, the Niger expedition of 1841 was supported by the missionary, and activist associations in Britain and the Government endorsed the effort to sign treaties with the native rulers, introduce Christianity and promote increased trade volumes. According to Dike (1962), the foundations of the Niger Mission were laid in this expedition of 1841[57]. He noted that the British Government commissioned its leaders to negotiate with important local chiefs and treaties for abolishing the slave trade, pointing out that the British Government was not concerned with trade alone[58]. In his paper, he documents:

> *In the instructions to the leaders of the expedition, the Government enjoined them to tell the rulers of Africa "that the Queen and the people of England profess the Christian religion; and that by this religion. They are commanded to assist in promoting goodwill, peace, and brotherly love, among all nations and men; and that in endeavouring to commence a further intercourse with the African nations, Her Majesty's Government are actuated and guided by these (Christian) principles[59]."*

The expedition berthed at Lokoja, at the confluence of Niger and Benue rivers. The group purchased land, cultivated a model farm, and not without the idea of setting up a centre for missionary work and trade[60]. By 1857, Dr. William Balfour Baikie, who led a successful expedition, once again reached Lokoja, acquired land, and signed a treaty with the Fula Emir. With Lokoja catching the British's eyes, it would become the outpost of Christianity in the Middle-belt and the North.

From 1841 to 1891, an era preceding the establishment of British colonialism in Nigeria, five principal missionary societies worked at where would become Nigeria as recorded by Ajayi (1965). The societies, according to him, included the Church of England; Church Missionary Societies (CMS); the Wesleyan Methodists Missionary Society, a committee of the English Methodist Conference; the Foreign Mission Committee of the United Presbyterian Church of Scotland; the Foreign Mission Board of the Southern Baptist Convention of the United States; and the Catholic Society of African Missions (Societe des missions africaines, S.M.A.) of France[61]. At Rabba, the erstwhile capital of Nupe Kingdom, Samuel Ajayi Crowther, an ex-slave of Yoruba descent, put up CMS's earliest missionary huts in the Emirate. He was amongst the British government-sponsored and Baikie-led 1857 Niger-Benue Exploration team. But Mohamman Massaba, who succeeded Usman Zaki later made up his mind and ordered both the missionaries and European agents out of Rabba to the confluence at Lokoja on the extreme edge of Nupe Emirate where it shares a border with the Igala kingdom[62].

One significant fact is that Nupe was an Islamic State, subject to the overlordship of the vast Sokoto Caliphate[63]. The Nupe Emirate's leaders were actually associated with what appears to be a popular Fulani's position holding that it was their duty to "dip the Quran in the sea[64]." F.J. Kolapo (2005) narrated the circumstance:

> *As the defender of the faith, it was Masaba's duty to uphold Islam's supremacy and spread it by jihad; his legitimacy and the legitimacy of the wars they had been fighting depended on the fulfillment of this role. Missionaries teaching Christian religion next to the court of the defender of Islam was clearly antithetical to this role*[65].

Although the CMS had made an appreciable effort to take Christianity to the middle-belt, which came under the influence of Fulani's Islamism, the more radical missionary group that would encroach the Islamic domain was the Sudan United Mission (SUM). The mission was founded by Hermann Karl Wilhelm Kumm (1875-1930) from Germany and his wife Lucy Evangeline Guinness (1865-1906). The first four SUM missionaries, Karl Kumm, John Maxwell, Ambrose Bateman, and John Burt, sailed on the "Akabo" for Nigeria on July 23, 1904. They travelled inland and were advised by the then High

Commissioner, Sir Frederick Lugard, that they should start work with the ethnic groups on the hill around Wase's town (in the present-day Plateau State). They travelled up the River Benue to Ibi and then headed north to Wase, about 80 miles from the river. Bateman developed appendicitis and had to return to England. Later, Maxwell and Burt trekked some 23 miles south of the River Benue to the town of Wukari, the centre of the Jukun people, and set up a mission station there[66]. Kumm would explain that:

> *"The whole raison d'être of the... mission is to counteract the Moslem advance among the Pagan tribes in the Benue region. This cannot be done by going to the Mohammedans, and therefore, our work will lie among the Pagan tribes[67]."*

The SUM, UK branch, was to focus on the Benue River area in Nigeria. The mission established bases at Rock Station in September 1904, including Wukari and Ibi in 1906. The Canadian branch also established three headquarters in Nigeria: Bida in May 1903, Patagi from January 1902, and Wushishi in December 1906[68].

SUM's Christianization of the Middle-belt and the North continued in 1907 and extended to Langtang among the Tarok (formerly called Yergum). Further expansion covered Berom, Sura, and Angas ethnic groups. In 1917, the first church was established in Donga. In later years the various branches of SUM set up additional mission stations in Northern Nigeria at Lupwe, Kona, Gandoile, Numan, Shillem, Pella, Lamurde, Bambur, Lantang, Tutung, Badung, Forum, Du, Vom, Randa, Lezin Lafiya, and Keana[69].

However, the history of the establishment of Sokoto Caliphate and the directive of Lord Lugard that the missionaries should confine their activities to only parts of the North where Islam was least thoroughly established transformed the Middle-belt into a fertile ground for Christian missionary enterprise, which set the stage for the future religious crisis in the North[70]. Christianity's presence in the middle-belt created an immense insulating force to further south the spread of Fulani Islamic influence. Since religion was often viewed as a symbol of ethnic identity, the insubordinate ethnic minorities in the middle-belt subscribed to Christianity to distinguish their identity from that of the Hausa-Fulani. Again, they saw Hausa-Fulani as usurpers and would punish them by not subscribing to their Islamic faith.

The adoption of Christianity and some middle-belters' quest to protect themselves from being Fulanized would further condition socio-political relations in the last decade of colonialism. In Jos in 1950, for instance, the first political association in the Middle-belt was formed. It acquired a Christian character, operating with the name the Non-Muslim League, but was subsequently renamed Middle Zone League (M.Z.L.). Its goal was to agitate for creating a separate state for the non-Muslim people of the Middle-belt[71]. Another group, Benue Freedom Crusade (B.F.C.), emerged and was stuck to the original idea of creating the state for only areas where Islam was less thoroughly established[72]. This, according to Akinyele (2004), "was the whole of Ilorin, Kabba, Benue and Plateau Provinces, the southern parts of Bauchi and Zaria provinces as far as Kontogora only, the Numan Division and Districts of Muri and Wurkum in Adamawa Province[73]."

To drive the point home, the ethnic minorities found in the northern half of Nigeria have challenged the Fulani system on all fronts. With these groups, the Fula agenda of pastoralism piety failed to gain free passage to the South. First, these ethnic minorities constitute major obstructions to the flourishing of the Fula culture of pastoralism as they would often convert the grazing lands to farmlands. They use massive cultivation of land as an economic weapon against Fulani's pastoral occupation. With desertification claiming much of available grazing space and the cultivation of food crops diminishing what is left for pastoralism, the stage is set for a reboot of Fulani jihad in the guise of herdsmen offensives.

Secondly, the ethnic minorities in the middle belt and the North, having formed multiple barriers against the spread of Fulanization to the Atlantic Ocean's shores in the South, also remained carriers of Christianity and de-Islamization agents in the region laid claim upon by the Fulani. These ethnic minorities use Christianity to exert their various ethnic identities. Communities whose members are predominantly Christians often see the Fulani as common settlers or aliens. It is also rare to see a Fulani who claims to be a Christian. By doing so, he vanishes his Fula identity. In the Northern region, where the Hausa language remains a lingua franca, religion becomes a veritable tool for identifying other groups from the Fulani. Therefore, the so-called herdsmen-farmers clashes in North Central Nigeria is more or less a war of identity flowing along the Muslim-Christian fault-line. The killings of farming communities are apparently a price paid by the ethnic minorities for resisting their conversion to the Fula identity by way of Islamization.

Finally, religious differences naturally influence the political support base. In Nigeria's prevailing political climate, religion determines loyalties. The Fulanis expect to garner support from the Muslim population. In this way, the ethnic minorities of the middle-belt are often viewed by the Fulanis as eroding their political support base. It would be recalled how the Fulanis violently attacked the ethnics of Southern Kaduna for not supporting their own Muhammadu Buhari in the 2011 presidential election but instead choose to support Goodluck Jonathan, a Christian from the South.

Meanwhile, the emirates' establishment has helped the Fulanis in no small measures to gain political advantage in modern Nigeria. For instance, in the modern-day Plateau State, the establishment of Wase emirate as an Islamic middle-belt enclave in 1820 following a successful jihad by Hassan, a Fulani from Bauchi, has today given the Fulani Wase Local Government Area and Wase Federal Constituency in a state dominated by various Christian ethnic nationalities. If the Fulanis were able to plant more emirates across Nigeria, the power derived from them would have yielded them more political fortunes - no thanks to the barriers imposed by the Islamic Old Kanem-Bornu Empire and the Christian ethnic minorities at the lower North. It seems the struggle for the soul of Fulani identity would continue with different manifestations in modern Nigeria as they keep their eyes on pastoralism, piety, and power.

CHAPTER FOUR

FULANI SYSTEM IN STRUGGLE WITH THE PROCESS OF NATION/STATE-BUILDING

Both classical and modern scholars have advanced explicit theories on the formation of a state. This ranges from natural concepts, social contract, voluntary, diffusionist, conflict, Hamitic, force, and several other theories one could think of. In as much as an effort would be spared in further theorization and assessment of existing conceptual frameworks of a state formation, this work will agree, to some extent with force or conquest theory in conceptualizing the emergence of Nigeria as a nation-state. The thesis of force theory is that the state is formed as a result of the subjugation of the weaker by, the stronger. Hence war is the sole factor for the creation of a state[1]. Until the 20th century, as we are aware, the territory known as Nigeria today did not exist as a nation. The process towards its creation commenced in the 19th century, and by the 20th century, the territory had taken the form and structure of a nation-state. According to Akpan (2004), "many ethnic groups numbering about four hundred in all were made part of the Nigerian nation. The process started with imperialism and ended with independence[2]."

The abolition of the slave trade by Britain in 1807, would play a significant role in the process of Nigeria's emergence as a nation-state. The very continuation of the slave trade by the dealers even after its abolition contributed significantly to the process that led to the country's formation. Onwubiko (1967) noted that "it was one thing to enact laws against the slave trade, and quite another thing to enforce such laws[3]." The British understood this situation. Onwubiko (1967) further advanced that, one of the ways by which the abolitionists thought the slave trade could be stopped was the substitution of legitimate trade in manufactured European goods and West African palm oil for the trade in human beings[4]." Again, he points out that Europeans thought it is necessary to explore the interior of West Africa to develop markets for the sale of manufactured goods and the purchase of raw materials[5]. In Akpan's (2004) submission in regards to enforcing the anti-slave trade, "Britain proceeded to bully, persuade or bribe other European nations, America as well as African chiefs to end the business, and with regards to Nigeria, the British began to negotiate anti-slave trade treaties[6]."

Akpan (2004) emphasized that the importance of the treaties was that once signed, the British used them as the excuse to bombard the indigenous states on the pretext that some articles of these treaties had been violated[7]. Ikime (1982) beams more light as he narrates that:

> *The bombardment affected, weakening the states concerned, forcing them to accept the superior might of Great Britain. It is clear, therefore that in retrospect the suppression of the overseas slave trade provided an indispensable prelude to the British occupation of Nigeria*[8].

Regarding the conquest of Fulani's Sokoto Caliphate, Bornu Empire and other groups in Northern Nigeria, the British government in 1821 began by sponsoring a southwards expedition from the Mediterranean coastal city of Tripoli through the Sahara Desert. The team reached the Bornu empire, becoming the first Europeans to reach Lake Chad in 1823[9]. Hugh Clapperton, a member of the expedition, explored further west of Bornu through Kano and the Hausa-Fulani territory to reach Sokoto. He reported back to Britain in 1825 as the quest to explore the interior of Africa continued to suppress the last vestiges of the slave trade by persuading the local rulers to sign treaties and to guarantee its traders access to the interior of Africa; Britain did this by sponsoring exploration from the south via Niger river. By the mid-nineteenth century, the British had already established a strong presence around the Niger-Benue confluence, including the river basins and adjourning areas.

In 1879, George Goldie advised the British trading enterprises to merge their business interests into a single United Africa Company (UAC). The merger helped Britain negotiate and conclude treaties with natives. The firm was later renamed Royal Niger Company (RNC) and was granted a charter to operate in the area. The difficulty of administering the vast and complex region came to the understanding of the government that the upriver territories, thus far entrusted to the Royal Niger Company should also be brought under central control. In 1900, the company's charter was revoked. Britain assumed direct control for the region from the southern coast to Sokoto and Bornu in the north[10]. Given British influence in the area, the entire axis had already been accepted at the Berlin Conference in 1884 as fallen to Britain in the Scramble of Africa. However, in the 1890s, there existed stiff competition between Britain and other European powers. To prevent Germany and France from occupying Northern Nigeria, according to Akpan (2004), "the British made up its mind to declare the area a British Protectorate. This aspiration was borne out of the fact that the British experienced stiff competition from the French[11]." Already by the 1890s, the French through its company, the Compagnie Francais de l'Afrique Equitoriale, had established stations and presence at Gbede, Lokoja, Egga, Shonga and Raba on the Niger and Ibi, Lokoja and Demsa on the Benue[12].

To actualize the proclamation of the Protectorate of Northern Nigeria, Britain in 1899 appointed Sir Frederick John Dealty Lugard as the High Commissioner. His first decisive move was to formally proclaim Northern Nigeria a protectorate on January 1, 1900, at Lokoja. Akpan (2004), narrated that "the Union Jack, a symbol of the British authority in the area was hoisted. The actions of Lugard tantamounted to a declaration of war on the peoples of Northern Nigeria[13]. Between 1900 and 1906, Lugard launched a series of wars to conquer northern Nigeria[14]. It was not long; the British forces subdued the Fulani empire and other defiant northern groups with the help of more sophisticated maxim guns. "Whatever happens we have got the Maxim gun, and they have not[15]," Sir Lugard had boasted.

By 1900 three protectorates existed: two in the south and one in the north. These were the Protectorate of the Southern Nigeria, the Lagos Colony and Protectorate, and the Protectorate of Northern Nigeria[16]. Northern Nigeria, in Akpan's account, was poor and unable to balance its budgets. It was dependent on imperial Grant-in-Aid which stood at £40,500.00 in 1905 and on the subsidy from Southern Nigeria Protectorate which stood at £75,000.00 in the same year.[17] By 1908, it became increasingly the view of many colonial officials that the amalgamation of the North and South was not only a sine qua non but a desideratum[18].

On January 1, 1914, the North and South were amalgamated, and a country known as Nigeria emerged. The British, by the application of force methods, were able to form a country by uniting differing ethnic groups with overlapping interests into one nation, thus making the task of nation-building to be extremely demanding.

The "3Ps" of Pastoralism, Piety and Power that formed the Fulani system's hallmark has been frustrated by the emerging Nigerian state which was initiated by the British colonialists. With the defeat of the Sokoto Caliphate in 1903 by the British, the Fulani imperial territory that was expanding towards the south and curved eastward below the Bornu empire into Cameroun lost its political power. Still, the Sultan title was spared for ceremonial functions.

British colonialism entered Nigeria by introducing restrictions to Fulani's agenda of pastoralism, piety and power that had hitherto flourished under the caliphate empire. The emergence of Nigeria has a role to play in impeding the Fulani system. The territory where cattle formed an integral part of the socio-economic or cultural life of its members, where Islam unites all social fabrics, and where the Fulanis hold the ultimate power to control the converted ethnics, became irredeemably upturned for a new nation-state to grow. It increasingly became a reality that, with the firm establishment of a modern state, the land would never revert to the status quo antebellum. This, notwithstanding, would not still deter the Fulanis from continuing with the pursuance of their agenda in a more pluralistic country that was born out of a marriage of convenience of some sort.

Pastoralism in Struggle

First, the pastoralist-agriculturalist conflicts in Northern Nigeria before the advent of British colonialism were not characterized by fatal confrontations. Some societies created social structures geared towards minimizing herders-farmers conflicts, thus preserving the overall harmony for their production symbiosis[19].

They had an official who regulates the grazing and pasture use of the herders' group. They were considered responsible for internal and external dispute management and settling conflicts between farmers and his group[20].

British colonialism came with formal laws and privatization of land which altogether brought a certain degree of restrictions to land use as well as alteration to the tenure system. Capitalism was fully entrenched as it encouraged an increase in the cultivation of cash crops for export to the industries in Britain which were known to be the workshop of the world. By 1950, according to Waller and Sobania (1994), "pastoralists had been relegated to the periphery of an economic and political system that was now dominated by the needs of export agriculture and in which stock had been bypassed for new avenues of accumulation[21]."

During the pre-colonial era, the land was deemed not owned by individuals but by communities and families in trust for all family members[22]. This form of land tenure system is known as a customary land tenancy. In pre-colonial times, the legal estate was vested in the family or the community as a unit. Since land ownership in the pre-colonial period was communal, the colonial authorities initiated laws and regulations governing land ownership, land use, and development amongst others to enable them to acquire and convey titles to land for the purposes of commerce and governance[23].

In 1900, the Land Proclamation Ordinance was enacted by the High Commissioner of the Northern Protectorate, Sir Frederick Lugard. According to Udoekanem, Adoga and Onwumere (2014) in their work, "the Land Proclamation

Ordinance was enacted to kill the institution of family and communal land ownership by facilitating the acquisition of title to land through the High Commissioner[24]." The taking over of lands by the British in northern Nigeria came with the promulgation of the Land and Native Rights Act in 1916 whereby all rights over native lands in Northern Nigeria were vested in the colonial Governor. According to Section 3 of the Act,

> *all native lands and right over the same are as a result of this declared to be under the control and subject to the disposition of the Governor, and shall be held and administered for the use and common benefit of the natives of Northern Nigeria and no title to the occupation and use of any such lands shall be valid without the consent of the Governor*[25].

With the formal laws introduced by the British colonial government, the Fulani had lost control of the land. The use of land, at that time, became subject to regulation. It resulted from the use of suitable pasture lands to whatever the government might deem a priority. The trend continued well into post-colonial time. From March 29, 1978, the Land Use Act, No.6 1978 was enacted by the military regime. Section 1 of the Act vested all land comprised in each state's territory in the Federation of Nigeria in the Governor of the state. Section 5(1) of the Act empowers the Governor of a state to grant statutory rights of occupancy to any person for all purposes in respect of land, whether or not in the urban area and issue a Certificate of Occupancy in evidence of such right of occupancy in accordance with provisions of Section 9(1) of the Act[26].

The Land Use Act of 1978 implies that governors in the 36

states and the Minister of the Federal Capital Territory take charge of the land tenure and enjoy the privilege of deciding on what could be done on any land in their territory. For the reason that the Act was primarily conceived to remove the impediment to infrastructural development, most state governments, especially outside the Hausa-Fulani domain, pay little or no attention to the provision of land for grazing. Outside states where Hausa-Fulani formed the majority, state governors would rather favour expansion in crop cultivation which often consumes the available land and leaves nothing for cattle grazing. The Land Use Act seems not to be protecting dry-season grazing lands known to the Fulani as Hurumi System which is observed by the pastoral Fulani. The system also lacks the legal statute to stop farmers from alienating the grazing land[27]." In this way, the Fulani herdsmen viewed their enterprise as being largely unprotected by the laws of the land. Consequently, they turned their contempt on farmers who appeared to be enjoying the benevolence of government. The takeover of the natural grazing areas by farmers, fencing of lands, and blocking of cattle routes (burtah) by modern infrastructures are primary causes that force herdsmen to take their cattle to farmlands for grazing. This is the primary cause of conflicts and even more, offers the foundation for other Fula agenda to creep in.

Although several governments have tried to prevent farmers from taking over all the available lands, the Nigerian state structure has served as a major setback to pastoralism. The British started in 1940 to separate the grazing land from the farmland but faltered because they, at the same time, imposed land-use control detached from economic and demographic dynamics in the pastoral system[28]. In 1954, there was a Fulani

Amenities Proposal which suggested the creation of grazing reserves, and by 1964, the government had gazetted about 6.4 million hectares of the forest reserve, 98% in the savanna. Sokoto province had 21% of the land, followed by Kabba, Bauchi, Zaria, Ilorin, and Katsina, with 11-15% each[29]. Reserves such as Wase, Zamfara and Udubo followed later.

In 1965, the government of Northern Nigeria incorporated the Fulani Amenities Proposal into the Grazing Reserve Law[30]. Then, the government created over 417 grazing reserves in the north[31]. But they have now been abandoned for no obvious reason other than the government's lack of commitment to the program's sustainability. In Nigeria, attempt to provide pastoral Fulani grazing reserve outside the States where cattle grazing is the mainstay often met with stiff resistance.

In 2016, Ekiti State enacted Anti-Open Grazing Laws followed in 2017 by Edo, Benue and Taraba States. The law was to ban open grazing owing to widespread killings, rapes, kidnappings, destructions of farmland and houses and other atrocities perpetrated on the pretext of grazing cattle. The secretary to Miyetti Allah Cattle Breeders Association of Nigeria (MACBAN), Saleh Alhassan said: "anti-grazing laws are nothing but populist agenda designed by visionless and desperate politicians to destroy our means of livelihood... these laws are oppressive and negative and are fundamentally against our culture as Fulani pastoralists[32]."

In Benue State, in particular, Governor Samuel Ortom enacted the state's Anti-Open Grazing Prohibition law which came into effect on November 1, 2017. Coming on the heel of this ban, the Fulani group converged in Kaduna. Those in attendance include Miyetti Allah Kautal Hore Fulani Socio-cultural Association; Tabital Pulaaku Nigeria Chapter; Miyetti Allah Cattle Breeders Association of Nigeria (MACBAN); Mobgal Fulbe Development Association; Pastoral Resolve (PARE) and Jonde Jam Fulani Youth Association. These pastoral groups published a communiqué which reads:

> *We (pastoralists) totally reject the repressive and oppressive 'Anti-Open Grazing Law' of Benue State as it is fundamentally going against our culture, economic interest and constitutional rights and we will deploy all the necessary legal means as enshrined in our Constitution to challenge it*[333].

Nonetheless, the pastoralists would not stop at that. They issued a warning that bore the semblance of threat.

> *We are appealing to His Excellency, President Muhammadu Buhari to call Governor Samuel Ortom to order as his actions are a fundamental threat to the peaceful coexistence and food security in Nigeria*[34].

The indigenous leaders in Benue State under the aegis of Mdzough U Tiv, Idoma National Forum and Ny' Igede responded that it was sheer mischief for the leaders of Miyetti Allah to ask President Buhari to call Governor Samuel Ortom to order because the anti-open grazing law was not made by Ortom but was a product of the people of Benue through their democratically elected representatives as a last resort in their futile effort to find peace and ensure the security of lives and properties in the state[35].

The Benue indigenous leaders believed that the open threat by the Fulani groups had led to the killing of 73 persons in Guma and Logo local government areas of Benue State on January 2, 2018, including the subsequent murder of two catholic priests and 17 worshippers at Mbalom parish in Gwer East local government area of the state[36].

Following the killings in Benue in January 2018, the then Minister of Agriculture and Ruler Development, Chief Audu Ogbeh, announced that the Federal Government of Nigeria would establish cattle colonies across the country to forestall bloodbath in the future. According to him, the cattle colony project would commence following the offer of five hectares of land by 16 states of the country, although failed to mention those 16 states. This announcement was subsequently greeted with widespread condemnation as a lot of commentators automatically saw it as a ploy by the federal government to seize lands and hand them to the Fulani herdsmen who would, in turn, use these lands as a springboard to colonize other ethnic nationalities in the country. Even the Taraba State Attorney General and Commissioner for Justice, Yusufu Akirikwen, mocked the cattle colony thus:

> *What is cattle colony? The colonial masters have colonized us, and now we will be colonized by cows*[37].

As if the policy label failed to strike the right chord, the Minister of Agriculture and Rural Development resurfaced yet again with another nomenclature called Ruga. The word, Ruga, is a Fulani term for Cattle Settlement, but it was phrased to mean Rural Grazing Area. On May 21, 2019, Audu Ogbeh said, "just ten days ago, President Muhammadu Buhari approved a programme called the Ruga settlement[38]." Explaining how Ruga works, the Permanent Secretary of the Federal Ministry of Agriculture and Rural Development, Mohammed Umar stated:

> *We feel that to do away with herders-farmers conflict; we need to settle our nomads and those who breed animals... We want to put them in a place that has been developed as a settlement, and we will provide water for their animals, pasture, schools for their children, security, agro-rangers, et cetera*[39].

The announcement of the Ruga policy was instantaneously greeted with condemnation by a lot of Nigerians. Some quarters saw it as a way of using cattle to aid Fulanis to penetrate all parts of the country. Most state governments kicked against Ruga. For example, Governor Kayode Fayemi of Ekiti State in the South-West said: "Nobody is coming to take our land in Ekiti; the governor of Ekiti State has power over the land of Ekiti, and it is the person that the governor gives land in Ekiti that can use the land in Ekiti[40]."

The Chairman of the South-East Governors Forum, Dave Umahi of Ebonyi State, gave an assurance that there was no plan to establish Ruga settlement in any part of the South-East and South-South zone[41].

In the Middle-Belt, the Benue State Government said it had made its stance known on the Ruga settlement matter, Benue would not be a part of the project[42].

In a statement signed by Most Reverend Emmanuel Chukwuma and issued at the end of the second session of its

17th Synod held in July 2019 in Enugu, the Enugu Diocese of the Anglican Communion said the Ruga settlement was the move to "impose the policy as an act of desperation by the Federal Government to unduly satisfy the wish of a particular ethnic group on the rest of the country[43]."

On Wednesday, July 3, 2019, concerned Nigerians heaved a sigh of relief when the Governor of Ebonyi State, Dave Umahi, announced that President Muhammadu Buhari had suspended the controversial Ruga program following the meeting of the National Executive Council (NEC) Committee on farmers/herders crisis. He said the program was not consistent with the NEC and Federal Government approved the National Livestock Transformation Plan (NLTP) which has programs of rehabilitation of internally displaced persons (IDPs) affected by the crisis.

Fulani Pious Culture in Struggle

Islam conveys a special identity to the Fulanis, and it is very rare to meet a Fulani who claims not to be a Muslim. The Fula's quest to expand their religious influence did not terminate with the political collapse of the Sokoto Caliphate or the introduction of the new system of governance by the British; instead, their Islamic interest was galvanized by competition advanced by Christianity. Since the government permits religious coexistence and accommodate their status parity, the Islamization by way of Jihad became discountenanced by the laws. Although the British defeated the Fulani's Islamic empire, the colonial administration which the colonists established in Northern Nigeria took serious cognizance of Islam[44]. The Muslim political institutions were used in the administration not only to protect Islam but also to make the British administration self-sufficient[45]. Sir Frederick Lugard prohibited Christian missions at emirates established axis but allowed entry only at non-Islamized areas. Despite the bias by the colonial government, Fulanization through Islamic tools were insulated by emerging political experiences that merged into the independence of a new nation. In post-colonial Nigeria, the law would not permit state-sponsored religion and would provide against intimidating, victimizing, or favouring anyone to influence their choice of religion. To promote secularity, Section 10 of Nigeria's Constitution provides that "the government of the federation or a state shall not adopt any religion as a state religion." Section 38 further reinforces individuals' rights to freedom of thought, conscience, and religion in its four sub-sections. Conversely, the same Constitution favoured Islamic religious article by providing in Section 275 the creation of state's Sharia Courts of Appeal. In contrast, Section 280 provides for the creation of state Customary Courts of Appeal.

Although the existence of the modern Nigerian state has attempted to water down religious domination, the Fulanis are still able to penetrate the Constitution with an Islamic agenda. As Pastor Bosun Emmanuel representing the South-West zone, admitted during the National Conference in 2014, the 1999 Constitution mentions 'Sharia' 73 times, Grand Khadi' 54 times, 'Islam' 28 times and 'Muslim' 10 times but does not mention the words 'Christ', 'Christian', 'Christianity' or 'Church' even once[46].

The Fulani have struggled in the post-colonial era to penetrate the system with Sunni Islam, which serves as a tool of their identity. The 1999 Constitution retained the 1979 provisions concerning the Sharia courts' jurisdiction, which has it that there could be state Sharia Courts of Appeal. Still, such courts were to be limited to civil proceedings and personal law concerning Muslims[47]. Alhaji Ahmed Sani, the then Governor of Zamfara State, announced in September 1999 that he would introduce a new expanded Sharia. According to Marshall (2005), the Sharia law he adopted covered the entire range of law and affected everyone regardless of religion. To date, despite continuing opposition from human rights groups and religious minorities, 12 of the 16 Northern and Central States have adopted an extension version of Sharia[48]. These states include Zamfara, Kaduna, Sokoto, Kebbi, Katsina, Niger, Kano, Jigawa, Yobe, Borno, Bauchi and Gombe. With the restrictions of Fulanization inherent in Nigeria's nation-building process, the Fulani might not rule out using herdsmen as a militant wing to achieve their jihadist agenda.

Fulani in Power Struggle

In the 19th century, the Fulanis exploited the weaknesses that were existing in Habe kingdoms, then staged a successful jihadist revolt after which they became the Caliphal overlords. When the British came, they also empowered the Fulani Caliphate to rule over other ethnics so long as they satisfied the interest and expectation of the British Crown. Fulani, being the sole controllers of emirates in the Caliphate, even to this day, enjoy residual power in manipulating the religiopolitical system to their favour. The Fulani have dominated the Northern system and could have entrenched their system in the country's body polity if not for the constitutional restrictions.

A huge threat to Fulani's power drive began with federalism when Arthur Richard's Constitution of 1946 created three regions, namely Northern, Western and Eastern Regions in Nigeria. The Mid-Western Region was created out of Western Region in 1966. With the creation of twelve states in 1967; seven in 1976; two in 1987; nine in 1991 and six in 1996, Nigeria now has thirty-six states. What this development means is that the Fulani population is divided or separated from their kith and kin into states within which they would form new associations and enter into new competition with divergent ethnic groups found in new distinct states. The only front where they could exert their hegemony remains at the federal level which serves as a platform for them to come together for synergy of interests and to effect Fula domination over the rest of the country.

There is the principle of Federal Character which stands to check the domination of one group over the other in Nigeria. As it would be recalled, the military regime of General Sani Abacha, a Kanuri from Kano, who sought to forestall political domination of a certain section of the country over others created Federal Character Commission (FCC) by decree in 1996. The FCC had been incorporated into the 1999 Constitution as one of the 14 independent federal executive bodies (153.1, Third Schedule Part 1). It has the mandate to work out the equitable formula, subject to the President's approval, for the distribution of posts in public service including political appointments. The distribution formula developed by FCC is strictly based on geographical areas including geo-political zones, states, local government councils and electoral wards rather than ethnicity[49].

President Muhammadu Buhari, a Fulani, has increasingly been pilloried as he is often viewed as making Fulani dominate in the power-sharing formula. This has heightened suspicion over perceived Fulani's quest to exert political hegemony on Nigeria's political system. In some quarters, there is a common belief that Buhari has subverted the Federal Character principles to give the Fulanis political advantage. In a statement by the National Christian Elders Forum (NCEF) on why Nigeria is increasingly suffering under the weight of insecurity, the group said: "the control of the military agencies mainly by Muslims from a particular part of the country was not only at variance with the Federal Character principle, it emboldens criminal elements to maim and kill innocent people in the guise of promoting Islam[50]."

The Middle-Belt Forum (MBF) on Wednesday, June 19 2019, while joining the fray to discuss insecurity in the country, said "there are many proofs to back up the NCEF's assertion that there is collusion between herdsmen and the Federal Government in advancing this campaign. In the past four years of Buhari's administration, tens of thousands of Nigerians have been decimated, with several thousand killed on account of Fulani herdsmen terrorist invasion of peaceful communities across the country. Despite the troubling death toll, none of the culprits has been arrested or brought to book[51]." The forum further stated categorically that the quest to subjugate other peoples in the country would be resisted.

> *The forum wishes to align itself completely with the position of the NCEF over ceaseless bloodshed that is deliberately founded on the orchestrated plan to eradicate and dispossess the peoples of the Middle Belt and Southern Nigerians of their ancestral lands and hand over same to marauding herdsmen terrorists. This plan to subjugate and conquer our people and Southern Nigeria will be vehemently resisted*[52].

CHAPTER FIVE

INSPIRATION OF KANURI-BASED BOKO HARAM INSURGENCY AS PART OF THE FULANI AGENDA

The establishment of a Sunni Muslim empire by the Fulanis following a series of jihads championed by Uthman dan Fodio in 1804 and his son, Mohammed Bello. They both had placed the Fulanis as one ethnic entity that stayed on top of the Northern system's Islamic religiopolitical ladder. At the same time, the Kanuri-led Old Bornu Empire bloc in the Northeast managed to play second fiddle role despite being unconquered by Uthman dan Fodio. Their confrontations from 1808 ended in stalemate producing two Islamic blocs in the North: Sokoto Caliphate, spanning Northwest to the North-Central (where Christian ethnic minorities impeded its spread to the South), while Old Bornu Empire of the Kanuri maintains the Northeast domain. Therefore, the insulation of the Sokoto Caliphate's expansionist drive by Muhammed Al-Kanemi's Bornu was not only fueling hostility between the two Islamic powers. Nonetheless plunging them into stiff struggles for religious, socio-political, cultural, and ideological supremacy in which the Fulanis still manage to have the edge over their Kanuri rivals.

The Kanuri-based militant group, *Jama'atu Ahlis-Sunna Lidda'awatiwal Jihad*, a description in Arab meaning People Committed to the Propaganda of the Prophet's Teaching, is known popularly as Boko Haram in Hausa language, meaning Western Education/Civilization is Sin. This Islamic sect evolved from the 1995 group operating under the name Shabaah which was then led by Mallam Lawal. When Lawal quit the group to continue with his education, a young Kanuri man, Mohammed Yusuf, took over the leadership. According to Musa Adziba Mambula, the new leader, Muhammed Yusuf, "was a charismatic Nigerian cleric who gained prominence among local youths in Maiduguri, the Borno State capital. By

2003, Yusuf led a movement espousing a conservative theology that mimicked Saudi-styled Salafism and opposed Nigeria's secular state which it considered corrupt and un-Islamic[1]." Yusuf officially founded the group intending to establish a sharia government in Borno State under the government of Senator Ali Modu Sherriff[2]. He built religious complexes in Maiduguri, which included a central mosque and a school where recruits were trained.

On June 11, 2009, as Mambula narrates, violence began when members of the police force clashed with mourners participating in a funeral procession. The funeral was in respect to some individuals who fell victim to an altercation that ensued between the police and motorcycle riders who violated the law on wearing safety helmets while operating motorcycles. As a result of the altercation, 17 of Yusuf's followers were shot by police officers[3]. Dozens of people were rounded up and executed with no trial; Yusuf's father-in-law was executed too, even as he was said not to have been a sect member. Joint Military Task Force engaged in excessive use of force, abuse, raids, burning of houses, and extra-judicial killings. This reckless brutality led Mohammed Yusuf to declare war on the Nigerian state, saying if the perpetrators have forgotten, the victims will not. With the uprising that followed, Yusuf was captured by the army and handed over to police, who summarily executed him outside the police headquarters in Maiduguri on July 30, 2009. A reprisal attack by Boko Haram followed, but the Nigerian security forces clamped down on Boko Haram suspects and sympathizers. The victims of the security brutality were majorly the Kanuri people. They suffered the rage of Nigerian security forces dominated by Hausa/Fulani and other ethnicities. Kanuri people had lost their loved ones, their properties, and their kith and kin were detained without trial. Against this backdrop, Boko Haram gained the sympathy and support of the wider Kanuri populace. The recruits joined the militant group not solely on religious reasons but based on pure ethnic sympathy and a quest to avenge their kinfolk's death. With endemic poverty stemmed from the Northeast region's marginalization at the time, the Kanuris saw nothing good in Nigeria.

Imbued with deep emotions for vengeance, Boko Haram transformed its credo from anti-Western rhetoric to a terroristic orientation, calculated at executing an Ethno-regional cum political agenda. Taking over Boko Haram's mantle of authority, Yusuf's right-hand man, Abubakar Shekau, a Kanuri from Yobe State, increased attacks both in frequency and intensity. The militant group became more sophisticated and organized in its approach to terrorism, killing tens of thousands of people, including security personnel and civilians. The sect's new leader, Shekau, took the insurgency to a virulent level. The administration of President Goodluck Jonathan mobilized a total of 100,000 security personnel to confront Boko Haram militants in the Northeast. In May 2013, President Jonathan declared a State of Emergency in Adamawa, Borno, and the Yobe States. The 7th division of the Nigerian Army was stationed in Maiduguri to take the fight to the insurgents in their enclaves. To give legal backing to war against terrorism, President Goodluck Jonathan approved, according to Section 2 of the Terrorism Prevention Act 2011 (as amended), the proscription of Boko Haram and authorized the gazetting of an order declaring the insurgents and terrorist activities illegal. Principal amongst the penalties was the death sentence of the insurgents, as well as the destruction of their domains. With the federal order, the Northeast was reduced to the war theatre where the Kanuris were visited with federal military might. The popular sentiment amongst the Kanuri populace became more ethnic than religious. Some saw Nigeria's security as Sokoto's Caliphate military wing.

Boko Haram carried out high profiled assassinations in Borno State before the 2011 general elections. Twin bombings in Abuja and Bauchi on May 29, 2011, when Goodluck Jonathan, a Christian from Southern Nigeria, was sworn in as the President of the Federation, claimed about 15 lives. Again, Boko Haram carried out a bombing attack on the United Nations headquarters in Abuja on August 26, 2011, where over 20 people were feared killed. These incidents became a loud announcement to the world, informing that a hitherto Kanuri-bred, ragtag militant group had become an internationally acclaimed terrorist organization.

The Kanuris, before the transformation of Boko Haram into a deadly terrorist group, did not have a mechanism set in place to aid them to advance their ethnic agenda like the Yoruba's O'odua Peoples' Congress (OPC); the Igbo Movement for the Actualization of the Sovereign State of Biafra (MASSOB), and the Ijaw Niger-Delta militants. Boko Haram became opportunistic and an available ethnic militancy tool for the Kanuris to use, like their counterparts in other sections of the country, to address the perceived imbalance in national opportunities and wealth distribution. Nonetheless, the Kanuri militants would later spur the Fulanis to produce their ethnic militia to pursue their 3Ps interests in the areas of pastoralism, piety, and power. Boko Haram would first arouse the Fulanis to adopt a protectionist approach, then motivate them to gang up against a Nigerian government headed by a Southern Christian. The Fulani's later reaction would be against Kanuri characters' sudden rise in the national politics under Buhari's government; hence, the need to offset the political equation once more.

Protectionist Drive

After the Federal Government descended heavily on Boko Haram in the second half of 2009, the militant group continued to carry out some level of attacks until their major operations in May and August 2011. Their subsequent activities reignited Fulani's suspicion that the Kanuri's Old Bornu Empire might be raising a fresh militant wing to redirect the course of history and move the Islamic supremacy from their Northwest domain to the Northeast. It appeared as if the Kanuris were taking the Fulani unawares. The Boko Haram Salafist doctrine of viewing the western way of life as sacrilegious and the sect's overt intention of establishing a Caliphate in Nigeria signalled to the Fulanis that a paradigm shift in the domination of the Northern system was imminent. The Sultan of Sokoto joined the fray in sneering at the sect and condemning Boko Haram as anti-Islamic and embarrassing to Islam. It was natural for the Fulanis who enjoyed the status quo in the Northern system to consider containment methods to the Kanuri disguised revolt.

With Boko Haram holding sway, fueling the Fulani's suspicion, the only mechanism for violence that could help reboot and protect the Fulani's agenda of pastoralism, piety, and power, remains the herdsmen. The herders were already in action from March 7, 2010, in religious clashes with Christian indigenes of

Dogo Nahawa, Shen, and Fan in Jos, Plateau State, where over 500 people were reportedly killed[4]. On March 17, 2010, the herdsmen slaughtered about 13 persons in Biye and Batem in Jos. On April 11, 2010, suspected Fulani herdsmen again attacked Berom communities. Here, the attackers targeted the homes of some officials in Kura Jenta. The apparent reason for the early 2010 attack by herdsmen in Plateau was that about 150 Muslims were allegedly killed and dumped in wells on January 19, 2010[5].

The scope of the Fulani's herdsmen onslaught at this period had centred more on the purpose of securing the area of influence, probably, to insulate the Kanuri militant's attack towards the Northwest and the North-central and to confine them to the Northeast. According to a report by Barkindo (2016), "at the height of the Boko Haram violent conflict in 2011, the Hausa-Fulani Muslim herdsmen took advantage of 'conflict environment' to launch attacks against Christian communities, particularly in the Middle Belt region of Nigeria, to conquer the territory[6]." This explains why it was of expedience to Fulanis to restart the expansionist-oriented jihad that was stalled by the European intrusion in the 19th century. The initial target was to secure the Middle-Belt, familiar territory, and a gateway to the South before the Kanuri agents gain a foothold.

On what changed the nomad-minded Fulanis to merchants of death, rape, and kidnapping, was hinted by Senator Dagiri Alkali, the leader of a delegation of The Miyetti Allah Cattle Breeders Association of Nigeria (MACBAN), to the Defense Headquarters, Abuja. As Akinyetun (2016) reported in the Asian Journal of Multidisciplinary Studies, Senator Alkali said the attacks carried out by the Fulani herdsmen were more of a necessity arising from the effect of the Boko Haram attacks in the North. The claim that Boko Haram insurgents attacked the Fulanis in the Northeast and other parts of the country, stealing many cows from the breeders[7]. The head of the delegation further emphasized that the herdsmen were acting in self-defense. He said: "But you as the military people, you know self-defense is an art. In the military, if you are attacked, you have to defend yourself. You have been squeezed; you have to find a way to survive[8]."

The capturing of territories and converting Christian ethnic minorities to Islam by the Boko Haram leader, Abubakar Shekau, riled the Fulanis. In August 2014, Boko Haram captured Gwoza, a mainly Christian community on Nigeria's Northeast border with Cameroun, and declared it an Islamic Caliphate. In a 52 minutes video made on Sunday, August 3, 2014, Shekau proclaimed:

"Thanks to Allah who gave victory to our brethren (in the town of) Gwoza and made it part of the Islamic Caliphate... Allah Used us to capture Gwoza; Allah is going to use Islam to rule Gwoza, Nigeria and the whole world[9]."

Gwoza was renamed by Shekau as Dar al-Hikma, meaning 'Abode of Wisdom.' Boko Haram went on to capture Mubi in October 2014. Mubi is a town in Adamawa State which has Gude Nzanyi, Fali, Kilba, Marghi, and Kamwe as major ethnic groups. More than half of Mubi are Christians. Late Alex Badeh, the Chief of the Army Staff at the time, was an indigene of Vimtim in Mubi. Boko Haram captured Mubi and subsequently renamed it, Madinatul Islam, meaning 'City of

Islam.' The sect held some areas in Adamawa up to Michika on the Cameroun border.

With Kanuri's Boko Haram seizing territories and seeking to establish Islamic Caliphate over Nigeria and the world, the Fulani's swift and forceful response contributed to the massacre of about 1,229 persons in 2014 alone. This was a way of protecting their area of control in the Middle Belt and sticking to whatever policy the Kanuri militants would bring to their domain. Therefore, the Fulani herdsmen violent conflict could be a way of warring to maintain the hegemony of the Sokoto Caliphate over the Old Bornu empire and suppress any Caliphate proposed by the agents of Kanuri interest.

Gang-Up Against Incumbent Power

With Dr. Goodluck Jonathan, an Ijaw Christian from the South, emerging as President of the Federal Republic of Nigeria in the 2011 presidential election, it became an open secret that the Islamic extremists detested his government in the North. Jonathan, who contested on the platform of the Peoples' Democratic Party (PDP), was declared a winner with 22,616,416 votes ahead of General Muhammadu Buhari (Rtd), a Fulani and a candidate of Congress for Progressive Change (CPC) who trailed with 12,250,853 votes. The Fulani's violent reaction to the outcome of the April 16 Presidential Election resulted in the killings and maiming of people in Kaduna and other states in the North. Before the elections, it would be recalled that prominent Fulani figures in the likes of Junaid Mohammed and Mallam Adamu Ciroma had made incendiary remarks threatening violence and suggesting national disintegration if they fail to have their way[10].

According to The Pivot Newspaper (2011) editorial, "as soon as more results indicated a sure victory for Jonathan, northern youths went on a rampage in a physical manifestation of their leaders' verbal thuggery and coded messages over time killing innocent souls and burning worship centres[11]."

The spate of killings by Fulani herdsmen increased steadily during Jonathan's tenure even though the herders didn't come on top in the ranking of the deadly world terrorist organizations until 2014, a period which preceded another electoral year. By 2014, there was intense politicking as the year ahead would offer another opportunity to maintain or change the government. The Fulani herdsmen killed about 1,229 Nigerians in the pre-election year and were ranked in the Global Terrorism Index as the fourth deadliest terrorist organization globally, outdone only by the Taliban, the Islamic State, and Boko Haram[12]. With Boko Haram insurgents slaughtering and capturing territories in the Northeast while the herdsmen intensified attacks in the Middle-Belt, Jonathan's government received heavy criticisms for its inability to manage insecurity in the country. The then newly assembled All Progressives Congress (APC) exploited the unfortunate situation to score reasonable political points against the incumbent PDP government. The Fulani herdsmen exacerbated the situation with their increasing offensives; thus, inducing fear that Nigeria might head to total destruction should President Goodluck Jonathan succeed in his re-election bid in 2015.

General Muhammadu Buhari (Rtd), who emerged in the APC primaries on December 11, 2014, promised change in all ramifications of Nigeria's political, socio-economic, and moral life in Lagos line with his party's mantra. His promise also included releasing Nigeria from the grip of terrorists that held the country to ransom. With APC embarking on an aggressive electoral campaign and gaining more massive followers in the North and the South-West, the popularity of Dr. Goodluck Jonathan waned miserably. Pastoralist-driven terrorism became one strategy employed by the Fulanis to aggravate insecurity and cause the rejection of a Christian Southerner, paving the way for a Muslim Fulani from the North to take overpower. Therefore, it was the contribution by the Fulani herdsmen to insecurity in 2014 that cost Jonathan's re-election. The Fulani herdsmen learned from Boko Haram how to use insurgency to cripple the government and reveal the system's inherent vulnerabilities and administrators, especially the security structures. Fulani militants also learned from Boko Haram how to acquire weapons and then understood how to defy security measures to move arms and ammunition to their targeted places. With the inspiration drawn from the Kanuri militants, the Fulani herdsmen were able to formulate their strategies to exacerbate the situation of insecurity in Nigeria and discredit the power. The result led to the defeat of President Goodluck Jonathan while lending victory to General Muhammadu Buhari (rtd) at the polls in the 2015 general elections. However, it was natural to think that the Fulani herdsmen militancy would fizzle out with Buhari's coming due to consanguinity, but that would never be in Buhari's first tenure and beyond.

Reaction to Kanuri Rise to Prominence in Buhari's Administration

The first thing to understand is that President Muhammadu Buhari's father, Hardo Adamu, was a Fulani from Daura in the present day Katsina State, who got married to Zulaihat, a Kanuri from Kukawa in Borno State. This parental background blessed Muhammadu Buhari with dual heritage from two powerful ethnic groups in Nigeria. This could also help explain why these two ethnic nations are becoming more important to his administration than most of the country's groups.

The Kanuris, although fighting an ethnic cause through Boko Haram militancy, had managed to regain lost grounds in the political equation of the Northern system and the national front. Clearly, President Buhari apparently adopted a placatory approach in minimizing the aggression of Boko Haram by way of placing Kanuri personalities in key defense and strategic positions. According to Eric Teniola, "one of the most discussed topics during the first term of President Muhammadu Buhari was his special relationship with the Kanuri[13]." To fuel his speculations was his inauguration of the North-East Development Commission (NEDC)[14]. In Buhari's first term in office, a handful of the Kanuri domain personalities in the Northeast occupied strategic offices. They included late Abba Kyari, Chief of Staff; Lt. General Tukur Yusuf Buratai, Chief of Army Staff; Major-General Mohammed Babagana Monguno, National Security Adviser; Ibrahim Magu, former acting Chairman of Economic and Financial Crime Commission (EFCC); Dr. Shettima Bukar Abba, acting Chairman, Federal Character Commission (FCC); Hon. Mustapha Baba Shehuri, Minister of State for Power, Works and Housing; Ahmed Kadi Amshi, Chairman, National Assembly Service Commission; Engr. Mustapha Y. Maihaja, Director-General, National Emergency Management Agency (NEMA), and many other directors-general, special advisers, and special assistants in the public service. Also, Babagana

Kingibe held no office but was highly visible as one of the key members of Buhari's kitchen cabinet.

There was always a rising Fulani suspicion that their kinsman, Buhari, whose mother is of Kanuri stock, shifted power to the historically rival Kanuri's Northeast Islamic bloc, which might bring the two sections on an equal pedestal. Pointblank, an online investigative news site in April 2017, published a quote from an anonymous political affairs analyst who pointed to Fulani's suspicion and worries over increasing Kanuri influence in Buhari's government:

> *Surrounding himself with Kanuris is a mark of absolute trust and confidence, while his approach to his kinsmen smacks suspicion and distrust*[15].

On why Buhari tended to engage the Kanuri in his administration, the online news medium submits that "Buhari, bearing in mind the Boko Haram debacle on the assumption of office and the legendary stubbornness of the Kanuri group, who usually pride themselves in the historical fact, they were never conquered throughout the 1000 years of existence of the Kanem-Bornu Empire before the advent of the Uthman dan Fodio jihad, concluded that his agenda might not be realizable without the support of the Kanuri[16]." Ahmed Joda, the Chairman of President Buhari's Transition Committee and a retired Permanent Secretary, was amongst the think-tank that formulated Buhari's plan for the administration but had to recommend a cautious and placatory approach towards the Kanuri[17]. The popular argument was that, since Boko Haram management centers around the Kanuri, it would be best positioned to tackle the insurgency once and for all hence, the appointment of Kanuris in strategic defense position[18].

Nevertheless, the appeasement methods of ending the Boko Haram insurgency had failed or partially succeeded, despite having the Kanuri placed in critical positions hoping that they would help resolve the Kanuri insurgency question. From year two of Buhari's second term in office, what was observed was a gradual shift of strategic responsibilities from Kanuris to the Fulanis. It was clear that the Fulani's quest for power control had yielded fruit by relegating the rival Kanuris from the forefront, but not to the background per se. By this time, the Fulanis reemerged the dominant force in Nigeria's political system. Buhari conceded the country's power structure to the Fulani's agenda. Below are the major strategic offices occupied by individuals of Hausa-Fulani extraction, the Islamic bloc of the defunct Sokoto Caliphate.

1. Muhammadu Buhari - Katsina State - President of the Federation/Minister of Petroleum
2. Ibrahim Tanko Muhammad - Bauchi State - Chief Justice of Nigeria
3. Abubakar Malami - Kebbi State - Attorney-General of the Federation
4. Ahmed Idris - Kano State - Accountant-General of the Federation
5. Danladi Umar - Bauchi - Chairman, Code of Conduct Tribunal
6. Ibrahim Gambari - Kwara State - Chief of Staff
7. Bashir Salihi Magashi - Kano State - Minister of Defense
8. Sidique Abubakar - Bauchi State - Chief of Air Staff
9. Maigari Dingyadi – Sokoto State – Minister of Police Affairs

10. Abubakar Mohammed Adamu - Nasarawa State - Inspector General of Police
11. Mohammed Umar - Kano State - acting Chairman of Economic and Financial Crimes Commission (EFCC)
12. Yusuf Magaji Bichi - Kano State - Director of DSS
13. Ahmed Rufai Abubakar - Katsina State - Director-General, National Intelligence Agency
14. Mohammed Sani Usman - Kano State - Chief of Defence Intelligence Agency
15. Ja'afaru Ahmed - Kebbi State - Comptroller-General of Nigeria Correctional Service
16. Mohammed Babandede - Jigawa State - Comptroller-General of Immigration
17. Hameed Ibrahim Ali - Bauchi State - Comptroller-General of Nigerian Customs Service
18. Hadiza Bala Usman - Kaduna State - Managing Director, Nigerian Ports Authority
19. Tukur Bello Ingawa - Katsina State - Chairman, Civil Service Commission
20. Mahmood Yakubu - Bauchi State - Chairman, Independent National Electoral Commission (INEC)

As noted earlier, the Kanuris are gradually losing top positions in Buhari's government to Fulanis. For instance, late Abba Kyari, former Chief of Staff who died of Covid-19 (speculated) in April 2020, was replaced with Dr. Ibrahim Gambari, a Fulani from Kwara State. Mohammed Umar, another Fulani from Kano, was elevated from the position of EFCC Director of Operations to replace the acting Chairman, Ibrahim Magu, a Kanuri man from Borno State. This change was effected following charges of corruption and insubordination preferred against Magu in July 2020 by the Federation's Attorney-General, Abubakar Malami. Instead of Magu's second in command and EFCC secretary, Olanipekun Olukoyede, a Yoruba man to get the top job, Umar's position was confirmed through an internal memo on Wednesday, July 8, 2020[19]. It was a mild development that reflected the Fulani power schema. Besides, some pundits in Nigeria were of the view that the insubordination aspect in Ibrahim Magu's case had a whole lot to do with Magu's insistence to bring to trial Senator Mohammed Danjuma Goje, a Fulani from Akko, Gombe State, who was accused of siphoning about N25 billion. Rumour has it that pressure came from the Attorney-General's office upon Ibrahim Magu to drop the charges. It seemed Magu had ruffled the sacred feathers with his own dirty hands; thus, he had to pay for it.

The Kanuris again had lost another important office when Buhari refused the elongation of Dr. Shettima Bukar Abba's tenure, a Kanuri from Borno, who was serving as the Chairman of the Federal Character Commission (FCC). He was subsequently replaced by Dr. Mrs. Muheeba Dankaka from Kwara State in April 2020. Notwithstanding, the highest positions the Kanuri were still managing to hold on to as at the time of this writing include the Senate President's seat occupied by Senator Ahmed Lawan, a lawmaker representing Yobe North in the Senate; Lt. General Tukur Yusuf Buratai still remained the Chief of Army Staff; Buhari still maintained Major-General Mohammed Babagana Monguno (Rtd) as his National Security Adviser, and Mele Kolo Kyari from Borno State still held the fort as the Group Managing Director of Nigeria National Petroleum Corporation (NNPC).

The Fulani's power advantages through Muhammadu Buhari's presidency were the fruits of ethnic militancy, which has precedence in Nigeria's contemporary history. As it would be recalled, the Yorubas in the South-west had formed a nationalist movement called O'odua People's Congress (OPC) led by Frederick Fasehun and Gani Adams in the 1990s to agitate against the annulled June 12, 1993, presidential election which was claimed to have been won by their kinsman, Chief M.K.O. Abiola who later died from suspicious circumstances on July 7, 1998. The OPC militancy majorly targeted the Hausa-Fulani living in the South-West while pressurizing the military governments for the Yoruba presidency. It was against this background that Chief Olusegun Obasanjo, a Yoruba man, was considered for a president's position when democracy eventually returned in 1999. After Obasanjo's tenure, the Ijaws in the South-South, through Niger-Delta militancy, got a vice-presidential slot as a pacifier, and their kin, Dr. Goodluck Jonathan, was chosen as a running mate to late Alhaji Umaru Musa Yar'Adua in the 2007 Presidential election. Jonathan then went ahead to become a substantial president following the death of President Yar'Adua on May 5, 2010. Jonathan further contested the 2011 presidential election and won against Buhari. Following that electoral episode, the Kanuris, using Boko Haram insurgency, and the Fulanis through herdsmen militancy played their ethnic cards in a way that produced Muhammadu Buhari as a president. President Buhari's father was a Fulani, and mother, a Kanuri.

Meanwhile, it has become an unwritten code in the contemporary Nigerian polity to employ ethnic militia in the agitation for power. Apparently, ethnic militancy in Nigeria would not go away anytime soon. Every ethno-sectional interest has now identified the need for an ethnic militia in competing for socio-economic and political goals in a pluralistic country such as Nigeria. Therefore, it is unfortunate that Boko Haram and herdsmen's violent conflicts would remain protracted so long as both Kanuris and Fulani's agenda persists. A Kanuri presidency in 2023 might resolve the Boko Haram insurgency, but it would likely birth ethnic militias in other parts of the country. Refusal to allow Kanuris a shot at the presidency means a likely continuation of Boko Haram militancy because the Kanuris from the Northeast believe they deserve to provide Nigeria with a president in the new dispensation of democracy.

Yet again, it seems the Fulani agenda might exist beyond Buhari's presidency. Next general elections in 2023 may still offer the Fulanis an opportunity to negotiate for another president's production. The Fulani's have a valid argument bordering the fact that presidents, since 1999, emerged from the Southwest, South-south, and Northwest. Therefore, it would be the turn of North-central, Northeast, and Southeast geo-political zones to produce subsequent presidents. Based on these geo-political arrangements, a Fulani can still emerge from Northeast or North-Central to contest for the presidency since zoning of positions is based on regions instead of ethnicity. Therefore, it is on this basis the Fulani would build their power agenda and go into the struggle for the highest political office in the country once more. Nonetheless, this could breed another set of ethnic militias.

CHAPTER SIX

CONCLUSION: RESOLVING ETHNIC AND CONSTITUTIONAL QUESTIONS

Fulani herdsmen killings, kidnappings, raping, robbing, plundering, burning down farming communities, and many other atrocious criminalities are not sparked by novel factors strange to Nigeria and Nigerians. These are the manifestations of the same old phenomena of ethnic rivalries. Ethnic-motivated violence keeps recurring in Nigeria's contemporary history, taking on different shapes; it blatantly seems unlikely to go away. For decades, the country has been rendered volatile and vulnerable due to the polity's cynical manipulation by captains of ethnic interests. Various commentators would not stop blaming the situation on the British colonialists' insensitivity who merged distinct ethnic nations, their overlapping interests, and their identities into one artificial nation-state. It, therefore, becomes natural to have pugnacious competitions amongst various groups of people. Situations of conflict arising from competition for incompatible goals and politics predicated on ethnic arrogance have over time led to mass death and wanton destruction of properties.

The seeds of discordant struggles among the ethnicities were sown in the past, and the succeeding generations are reaping the fruits in the form of violent conflicts and deprivations. As noted by Akinyele (2004), many opinion leaders have attributed the roots of all the crises bugging the country to the process of unification, particularly the amalgamation of 1914[1]. According to Crowder (1978), "the union was so sudden and included such widely different groups of people[2]".

A handful of scholars do not totally build their belief around the ethnocentricity of Nigeria's problem; instead, they blame the ruling class for employing ethnic orientations in manipulating the system to their interests. Hale (2008) saw ethnicity as a mere "spin" that politicians put on events to mask their motives, usually alleged to be greed or political ambition[3]. In the like manner, Sule-Kano (2015) opined that the politics of ethnic identities in the struggle for political power in Nigeria was rooted in some ideological and political character of the dominant class[4], and therefore concluded that the degenerating condition of the Nigerian state, which involved the decomposition and disarticulation of effective state authority and legitimacy had nothing to do with the genes of ethnicity in Nigeria[5]. In theorizing the origins of ethnic-oriented conflicts, Cohen (1978) pointed out that identifying an ethnic group was more socially- and politically-motivated. The socio-cultural and behavioral differences and people of different ethnicities do not necessarily stem from inherited traits and tendencies derived from common descent[6].

The preceding commentaries point out that ethnic consciousness and identity are empowered by the dominant power-class who employ ethnic sentiments to further their ambition. Regarding Northern Nigeria, the Islamic religion has been activated as a means of identifying differing groups from others and the tool used by the power class for empire building. This eventually becomes problematic to the process of nation-building. Dahiru (2020), in his Out of The Box column of The Sun Newspaper, clearly captured the origin of how ethnic elites in the North employed Islamic tools for power ambition, tracing it down to the death of Prophet Mohammed, PBUH:

Upon the death of the Prophet of Islam, Muhammad, PBUH, in 632 AD, his companions developed and incorporated certain doctrines into mainstream Islamic theology to maintain unity and cohesion of the early Muslim community. To legitimize a centralized rule over the fledgling Muslim community, which had developed in Medina's city under the divinely guided leadership of the Prophet of Islam, and command absolute loyalty from the Ummah, the doctrine of Caliphacy was introduced into Islamic theology. Caliphacy essentially entails a Unitarian Islamic State governed as a theocracy with Quran as exemplified (Sunnah) by the Prophet of Islam as the legal framework (Sharia) under the leadership of his acclaimed successor, designated as the Caliph... Having achieved a semblance of unity of the early Muslim community under the Caliphacy, Muslim rulers soon went from religious leaders and guardians of faith to empire builders. To advance their worldly cause of dynastic empire building, a religious justification had to be sought. To expand the boundaries of the Muslim state outside Medina's precincts to the Judeo-Christian lands of Egypt, Damascus, Jerusalem, and Constantinople, a doctrine that reclassified believing peoples of the Book (Christian and Jew) as unbelieving enemies of Muslims had to be evolved. The reclassification of the people of the Book as outright unbelievers, henceforth, legitimized expansionist aggression against people of other faiths by empire builders as a noble struggle in the cause of the spread of God's religion (Jihad)[7].

When the elitist Fulani class were seeking to seize power from the Habe rulers, Islamic religion became a veritable tool in mobilizing support and waging a jihad to oust the reign of the Hausa rulers whom the Fulani Islamists viewed as being impious or outright pagans. After rounds of successful jihads came the establishment of the Fulani empire called Sokoto

Caliphate. The distribution of power then centered on the Fulani elitist class and warriors who solely enjoy the Emirs' office in the permanent exclusion of other ethnic Muslims. The bottom line is that it is the Fulani power class that inspires ethnic nationalism, including the pulaaku spirit of ethnic supremacy and the call to ethnic assertiveness. The Islamic identity then serves not as an end in itself but as a vehicle to convey the Fulanis power agenda and impose it on Nigeria. Even in the modern Nigerian state, the Fulanis still find Islam as a means to convert other ethnic groups and to relegate their worldview and interests to the substratum of Fulani pastoralists, piety, and power agenda.

The political elite in Nigeria has somehow stirred ethnic nationalism and used it to their advantage. All of these, at the detriment of the nation-building process. Ethnic nationalism defines groups by a shared heritage, which usually includes a common faith and common ethnic ancestry[8]. Aluko and Ajani (2009) stressed that "political actors tend to emphasize our diversity and those things that separate us rather than emphasizing things that unite us[9]." Therefore, one of those things that separate groups in Nigeria are the religion. Over time, this has served as an easy tool employed by political elites in deepening cleavages between various ethnic nationalities in Nigeria.

One precarious circumstance surrounding Nigeria as a nation-state is its citizenry's switch of national patriotism to ethnic's loyalties. Aluko et al. (2009) emphasized this point while commenting on the origin of ethnic militias in Nigeria:

> *In real life, an ethnic nationalist identifies with and sees himself or herself first as a member of a particular ethnic nationality before identifying themselves with a nation. Thus, this helps to explain the emergence and proliferation of ethnic associations and militias...*[10]

Nkolika (2007), in her work, lamented that Nigerian citizens were torn between loyalty to the Nigerian state and the loyalty to the in-group movements manifesting today as ethnic militias[11]. As observed, rallying around what is perceived as an ethnic cause by ethnic nationalities has strengthened the operations of ethnic militias in Nigeria. For instance, the Kanuris in Chad, Cameroun, and Niger has reportedly been invited by their kin in Nigeria to cross over to lend force to the Boko Haram insurgency. Similarly, Fulani herdsmen from neighbouring African countries have also reportedly been ushered in by their Nigerian counterparts to wreak carnage on other ethnic nationalities in the country. The motive why both Kanuri and Fulani militant formations enjoy surplus human resources as they cut a swath through the vast area of the Nigerian territory is not that their population in the country overwhelm others. Still, it is because their kith and kin from neighbouring African countries cross over to rally support for their fellow ethnic stock in Nigeria.

Nonetheless, on some occasions, the Fulanis in Nigeria would come to deny culpability while shifting the blame on non-Nigerian transhumant herdsmen. Speaking with journalists in July 2017, MACBAN Assistant National Secretary-General, Ibrahim Abdullahi (2015), rapped the Federal Government for leaving porous borders, saying it is responsible for free entry and exit of the killer herdsmen, mostly foreigners[12]. According to him,

> *in Nigeria, our borders are porous; people come in anytime and go out anytime they want, In fact, it is a shameful thing today that we don't even know those that are indigenous Fulani or trans-human Fulanis*[13].

Abdullahi (2015) went on:

> *Another problem we have that you people don't know is that these migratory Fulanis come with all forms of weapons... Some of these countries that Fulanis come from in Africa have crises like Chad and the Central African Republic, where there is rebellion*[14].

However, Abdullahi (2015) did not explain how AK-47 wielding foreign herdsmen would understand the terrain, detect and avoid Muslim and Fulani areas in Nigeria while wreaking havoc on indigenous Christian communities without taking directives from the indigenous Fulani in the country. This suggests that the Fulanis in Nigeria might have invited their kith and kin in the Central African Republic that were displaced by the instability arising from Muslim-Christian conflicts since 2014, to cross over and join the struggle for more grazing space in Nigeria. Most of the affected Fulanis in the once turbulent Central African country might have passed through Nigeria's porous border with a large cache of firearms to help prosecute an ethnic cause. Therefore, this background, in a way, could support the argument that the Central African Republic crises have given vent to the proliferation of weapons that eventually found its way to Nigeria, giving the Fulani herdsmen the upper hand over their ethnic rivals. The MACBAN Assistant National Secretary-General had to confess that in Chad or the Central African Republic, where there was an occurrence of rebellion, "weapons have become like pure water or bread, so people from there see it as normal to hang AK-47[15]."

As northern Nigerian borders are left bare to foreign intrusion, to bring into the country assorted kinds of weapons, ethnonationalism would continue to find expression in violence, thereby posing a serious threat to the Nigerian state's existence. Abdullahi emphasized the need to understand all kinds of Fulanis available in the country in a bid to identify the migrant herdsmen who illegally enter Nigerian territory to perpetrate criminalities. According to him, the Fulanis are categorized into three:

> *Once you have the settled Fulanis (in) every part of the North you have Fulanis indigenous to that area. Then you have the semi-settled Fulanis. They move, but the movement is not constant and is not very far. Then you have the trans-human Fulanis. Those that are constantly on the move and can also be categorized into two. Some of them are Nigerians, while some are foreigners from neighbouring countries like Cameroun, Chad, and even Niger*[16].

The Fulani herders' assistant scribe did not only stop at identifying categories of his ethnicity. He advised the government on measures to adopt in tackling the nomad pastoral menace prevalent in the country. In his words,

> *'Neither Nigeria opts out of the ECOWAS (Economic Community of West African States) protocol, nor should we apply the conditions. We should ensure that anybody coming into the country knows when he is coming, where he is going, and control what they are coming with. For example, if you are to move from Niger to*

Nigeria at the border, there must be what we called Control Posts. So, it is left for the government to do the right thing, let us decide who comes in because it is our country, let us decide the terms for the person coming. Let us not because ECOWAS protocols leave everything to fate. That is not going to help us... The truth is that when you go to your village today, you will see Fulanis that have been there since. Apart from the knife and stick they have and maybe a Dane gun for hunting, they don't have an AK-47. The truth is these people coming from other countries we have to control them[17]*."*

At the state level, Thomas (2019), the Executive Director of Foundation for Civic Education, Human Rights and Development Advancement (FoCEHRaDA), suggested that the state government take a census of herdsmen state to be able to monitor their activities at all times[18]. In his words, "the state government should take a census of nomadic herdsmen, understand the locations they are, and monitor their movement from one point to another[19]."

However, Fulani's ethnicity seemed to convey upon herdsmen special privilege that they go about with firearms. At the same time, other nationalities would not dare without incurring the wrath of the Nigerian security. Bearing of arms by Fulani herdsmen without recourse to laws and security prohibitive measures had considerably peaked suspicion from a large section of the Nigerian public who see officials' attempt to entrench Fulani ethnic supremacy in modern political and governmental structures. The Fulani herdsmen continue to operate with impunity, the Middle Belt Forum (MBF) and Nigerian Christian Elders' Forum (NCEF) insisted that there is a collision between herdsmen and the Federal Government in advancing this campaign[20]. Amongst prominent personalities that also shared this thought was the former President, Chief Olusegun Obasanjo, who raised the security stakes by alleging plans by some extremists to Islamize and Fulanize the West African sub-region[21]. In May 2019, President Muhammadu Buhari was accused of double standards in dealing with the security challenges posed by unlawfully armed herdsmen who had become a national menace as he gave a presidential order revoking duly issued licenses to bear arms[22]. As voiced out by The Nation Newspaper columnist, Amalu (2019), "those who are terrorizing the citizens, whether as kidnappers, highway robbers, cattle rustlers, armed herdsmen, and sundry bandits do not require license to bear arms. So, those who will be affected are law-abiding citizens who have taken administrative measures to stay within the law by applying for a license to own guns[23]." Those opposed to the directive even argue that the presidential order was to give advantage to the armed herdsmen they believe the President had sympathy for[24].

Claims of Fulani herdsmen who openly brandish their AK-47 without being arrested by the Nigerian security have continued to cast aspersion on the government's sincerity in tackling insecurity in Nigeria. Mr. Aondoaka Ugoh, a resident of Tse Dzungwe settlement, Mbakprya, Mbaiwen in Tombe Local Government Area of Benue State, after fleeing his home following the takeover of the entire area in March 2020, by armed Fulani herdsmen, recounted to The Nation. How herdsmen armed with AK-47 and large herds of cattle grazed their cows freely in the area, destroying farmlands and eating up the harvested crops[25]. The incident occurred when the Benue State government outlawed open grazing in the state, yet security operatives seemed to look the other way.

Most pundits still wonder why the wrath of the law has not caught up with the herdsmen over the illegal possession of arms despite the fact that, in Nigeria, there is the Firearm Act, Cap 146, Laws of the Federation 1990. The law generally provides that to bear arms, one must obtain a license. Section 3 provides that "no person shall have in his possession or under his control any firearm of one of the categories specified in Part 1 of the Schedule hereto (starting now referred to as prohibited firearm) except in accordance with a license granted by the President acting in his discretion.[26]"

Section 4 further provides: "no person shall have in his possession or under his control any firearm of one of the categories specified in Part II of the schedule to this act (starting now referred to as a personal firearm) except in accordance with a license granted by the Inspector-General of Police which licenses shall be granted or refused in accordance with principles decided upon by the National Council of Ministers[27]." Nonetheless, it seems the foregoing provisions do not apply to the Fulani ethnic herders.

In its criticism, The Punch Editorial Board, in January 2018, pointed out that "by law, it is a crime to carry unlicensed arms, but the security system is so dysfunctional and compromised that Fulani herdsmen openly clutch lethal weapons[28]." Hence, the failure of the security agencies to stop them bespeaks official complicity in their genocide[29]. In a like manner, the Igbo socio-cultural organization, Ohanaeze Ndigbo, in March 2020, accused law enforcement agencies of ignoring reports of herdsmen moving around with AK-47 rifles in a community in Anambra State[30]. In a petition to the Inspector-General of

Police, Mohammed Adamu, dated March 3, 2020, and entitled, The Road To Anarchy, and signed by Nnia Nwodo, the President-General of Ohanaeze Ndigbo. The group alerted the Police that the Umuawulu community's residents in Awka, South Local Government Area, had sighted four 'herdsmen' with AK-47 rifles slung on their shoulders on their way to Isiagu community where they reside[31].

The letter reads in parts,

> *When the news of the brazen wielding of firearms spread across the council area, as law-abiding citizens, stakeholders there convened a crucial meeting with the Police and Fulani leaders and raised the matter for deliberation. The stakeholders told the Fulani leaders in the presence of men of the State Investigation and Intelligence Bureau (SIIB) Awka that they were alarmed and surprised that their boys were flagrantly displaying arms in the public, unmindful of the legal implications of unlawful possession of firearms... The stakeholders expressed disappointment that security agencies did not make any attempt to arrest the offending Fulani boys, adding that if it were Igbo boys, they would have been arrested, tortured, and charged to court. But rather than explain what led to the boys' carrying of arms or even apologize on behalf of the boys, the Fulani leaders told the stakeholders to do their worst. They walked out on them, saying that their boys must always bear arms to protect themselves against religious, ethnic, or tribal attacks from any quarters, and there is nothing anybody can do. This is the presence of law enforcement agents. Nothing was done to arrest either the Fulani boys or their leaders for overtly declaring war on the people of Anambra State*[32].

The Igbo group's President-General would further wonder if the bearing of "unlicensed firearms" is no longer illegal in Nigeria, querying, "do we now have different laws for different ethnic groups in Nigeria[33]?" He further asked: "If it were to be members of Independent People of Biafra (IPOB) or any other group other than Fulani that bear such illegal arms, what fate would befall them[34]?"

Other groups in the country would not fold their arms to watch as they were being threatened and gradually decimated by the Fulani ethnic militants. Their suspicion of government complicity is apparently increasing steadily, as the Federal Government does little or nothing to protect them in their communities against criminals and marauding herdsmen. Against this background, all governors from the six predominant Yoruba States in the South-West comprising of Ekiti, Lagos, Ogun, Ondo, Osun, and Oyo came together on January 9, 2020, to inaugurate Operation Amotekun. This security outfit would guarantee security for the region. This swift decision was expedited following the suspected Fulani herdsmen's murder of Mrs. Funke Olakunrin, the second daughter of Pa Reuben Fasoranti, the Afenifere leader. On Friday, July 12, 2019, the incident took place between Kajola and Ore along Ondo-Ore Road.

The inauguration of Amotekun won massive support across Yoruba ethnicity. The leader of the Coalition of Oodua Self-Determination Group (COSEG) said:

> *We are unreservedly in support of our governors for the proactive steps to put together AMOTEKUN, a community policing outfit, to*

ensure our people's safety. We use this opportunity to make a plea to our governors not to give in to conspiracy and deliberate attempt to scuttle their noble actions. You have acted in line with UN Resolution Article 51. Under customary law, anticipatory self-defense is permissible when the threat of an armed attack is 'imminent.' The Charter codifies the pre-existing customary rules of self-defense as a statutory right, not to limit it. The Nigerian security system has demonstrated that it has no answer to the recurring kidnapping, rape of our women, killing of farmers, and other societal ills that ravage our land. Hence AMOTEKUN was long overdue[35].

Conversely, the establishment of this Yoruba security outfit was sneered at by the Fulani personalities both inside and outside the government circle. Individuals like the ex-governor of Zamfara State, Alhaji Abdulaziz Yari, saw the establishment of Amotekun as an opportunity to dismember Nigeria. "According to him, "prominent Yoruba political leaders used the opportunity to make some divisive comments and call for dismemberment of Nigeria over the murder of the lady[36]". Besides, the six-state governors of the South-West geopolitical zone were summoned by the presidency prior to the inauguration of Amotekun. However, the launching of the outfit still went ahead to hold on January 9, 2020. Amidst wide condemnation from the North, the Minister for Justice and the Attorney-General of the Federation, Abubakar Malami, through his Special Adviser on Media, Dr. Umar Gwandu, via a statement issued on January 14, 2020, declared Amotekun illegal[37]. Malami argued,

"The Constitution of the Federal Republic of Nigeria 1999 (as amended) has established the Army, Navy, and Airforce (sic),

including the Police and other numerous paramilitary organizations for Nigeria's defence. No other authority at the state level, whether the executive or the legislature, has the legal authority over the defence[38]."

Replying to the Attorney-General of the Federation, OPC chieftain, and the Aare Onakakanfo of Yorubaland, Gani Adams, berated Abubakar Malami in a letter published in The Nation Newspaper edition of Friday, January 20, 2020, saying he serves as the Attorney-General of the country, not a section of the country[39].

Adam further fires at Malami thus:

Your outburst against the governors who were elected, not selected or appointed, is against the spirit of the 1999 Constitution (as amended). The right to life is universal, and no government can legislate against that. I don't need to border you about killings, kidnappings, banditry, and other criminal vices in the Southwest recently. Even as Mrs. Funke Olakunrin, the daughter of Yoruba leader, Pa Reuben Fasoranti, was killed. One thing is sure: Nigerians have the right to protect themselves against attacks. Amotekun is an initiative by the Southwest governors to defend our people. Where you are getting it wrong is this: the Amotekun initiative has nothing to do with the territorial integrity of Nigeria. If there is a breach of the country's territorial integrity, the military will come in immediately. So, nobody is rising against Nigeria. Your letter to the governors directly or indirectly implied that our people no longer feel safe because the land has been invaded by some elements from within and outside the country[40].

Another important Southwest socio-cultural organization that joined the fray was the Yoruba Council of Elders (YCE). The group condemned the Attorney-General's position on Operation Amotekun, describing it as a coup against the Yoruba nation[41]. Also, COSEG leadership said, "more worrisome but laughable was Malami's boldface of drumming colorful ethnic songs and marimba bigotry[42], adding that, "Malami can close his eyes to Isbah of the twelve northern states, the Civilian JTF in the northeast, but is now issuing an unconstitutional, malicious, divisive, but meaningless and unenforceable ban on Amotekun[43]".

Outside the Yoruba ethnicity, another organization that backed Operation Amotekun against Malami's discountenance was the proscribed Igbo group, the Independent People of Biafra (IPOB), from the Southeast. The group's leader, Mazi Nnamdi Kanu, in a broadcast on Thursday, January 16, 2020, said that the final and definitive stance of 'the Biafran people' was that IPOB would support Operation Amotekun with all its might[44]. It becomes a typical Nigerian scenario where ethnicity finds expression in militia formations and inter-group realignment. The establishment of Amotekun became contagious in stirring the yearnings for community-based security structures, homogenous to various ethnic groups as a way of resisting aggressive Fulani encroachment on Southern Nigeria. The Igbo National Congress (INC) has expressed disappointment over the failure of the Southeast governors to establish a regional vigilante force akin to Amotekun, announced to the press on June 15, 2020, through its National President, Godsent Chilos, that the group has launched a security outfit called Operation Lion Walk to secure farmlands and forests in Igboland and to protect Igbo farmers from armed Fulani herdsmen.

Similarly, governors of the South-south geopolitical zone while meeting on March 5, 2020, at Asaba, Edo State capital, to revive BRACED commission comprising of Bayelsa, Rivers, Akwa Ibom, Cross River, Edo, and the Delta States, resolved to set up a regional security outfit like Amotekun of the Southwest to compliment the effort of the Police and other security agencies in the task of policing the region[45], from armed Fulani herdsmen attacks. With the yearnings for community-based security arrangements in the South, it becomes clear that rival ethnic groups are prepared to contain ambitious Fulani ethnics' aggression. A scenario, as this prompted Prof. Wole Soyinka to say, during the 50th anniversary of the end of the Nigerian civil war, has it that the prevailing fragile state of the polity reminded him of the mid-1960s, just before the civil war[46].

Similar to how hyper-ethnic tensions led to the outbreak of the civil war in 1967, the Fulani herdsmen aggression could trigger another civil war, especially, as ethnic groups now tend to be considering breeding their in-group security outfits, having viewed the national security formations as being hijacked by Muslims and Hausa-Fulanis of the North. Based on common historical experiences, wars do not always erupt abruptly but would have to pass through a couple of processes where groups form alliance systems and security networks. If the Federal Government of Nigeria fails to disentangle itself from the web of ethnic biases, then Nigeria's teething problems would continue to bedevil the country or plunge it into cataclysmic inter-ethnic confrontations.

Assigning governmental and political portfolios asymmetrically in a multi-ethnic nation as Nigeria does not help achieve unity in diversity but rather increases ethnic tension and suspicion. The lopsided appointments by the Federal Government without taking into consideration the divergent interests and aspirations of the variegated ethnicities in the country have contributed in no small measure in compounding Nigeria's insecurity woes. According to NCEF (2019), the control of the military agencies mainly by Muslims from a particular part of the country was not only at variance with the Federal Character Principle. Still, it emboldened criminal elements to maim and kill innocent people in the guise of Islam[47]. On this ground, eminent socio-cultural leaders from the Southern and Middle-Belt sued President Muhammadu Buhari for N50 billion over the marginalization of the people of the regions in the appointments to security quasi-security agencies and "strategic agencies" of the Nigerian government. The 16 plaintiffs filed the suit marked FHC/ ABJ / CS/ 595 / 2020, at the Federal High Court in Abuja on June 8, 2020[48].

However, to resolve Nigeria's ethnic question, the first step would be to unravel the Northern ethno-religious factor that permeates the whole country. In the first place, the North, despite its seeming monolith outlook, also comprises multi-ethnic groups contending to be freed from the Hausa-Fulani system's facade. The majority amongst these varied groups include the Kanuri, Jukun, Nupe, Gwari, Tiv, Idoma, Berom, Marghi, Bassa, Chibok, Gade, Gwandara, Kambari, Ninzam, Saya, Shuwa, and scores of others. The Kanuri has used Boko Haram militancy to renegotiate their position in the northern system and Nigeria itself; consequently, the Fulanis have reacted by fueling herdsmen attacks on other ethnic minorities. In a bid to contain Boko Haram's influence within the framework of their 3P's agenda and, by extension, sort to maintain the status quo of the northern power equation. This emerging situation could spur other ethnicities to champion their own breed of insurgencies to get the Federal Government to pay attention to their fundamental challenges or be taken seriously in the affairs of the nation. This, as we all can see, could be a sure road to anarchy.

As major ethnic groups with a remarkable history of Islamic presence and practice in Nigeria, the Fulanis and Kanuris do not portray good examples for other ethnic entities to emulate. Rather than strive to show others the peaceful culture of Islam, they emphasize the jihadist-driven empire-building aspect, which is grossly at variance with modern-day realities of nation-building and democracy.

A remarkable observation was made in a newspaper by Majeed Dahiru, which generally pointed out that the quest for empire-building using Islamic radicalism has gone out of fashion. At the same time, nationalism now finds appeal in the territories of former notable Islamic Caliphates. Using the Ottoman empire and its succeeding nations as examples, Dahiru has been able to remind captains of empire-building enterprise in Nigeria that the old jihadist methods of expansionism have expired in the face of nationalism and democratization. He writes:

> *Whereas the twin doctrines of Caliphacy and Taqfiri and the reclassification of the believing, One-God-worshipping People of the Book as outright unbelievers are not Islamic. Still, only a Muslim invention for the purpose of empire building, they nevertheless are the most entrenched doctrines of mainstream Islamic theology in*

contemporary times. Following the collapse of the Ottoman empire in 1924, they were signaling the end of the over 12 centuries-old Muslim Caliphacy, a wave of nationalism swept through its successor nation-states of modern-day Turkey and those of the Middle East and North Africa. The emergent nation-states from the Ottoman Empire's rubble fiercely protected their territorial integrity by elevating the state's citizenship over cross-border pan-Muslim solidarity. To achieve this, these governments took proactive steps to rid their mainstream Islamic theology of any strand of doctrinal imprints of ancient empire builders, especially as concerns the concept of the Caliphacy, through a purposeful regulatory framework. This is precisely what Nigeria has failed to do so far. Unfortunately, this has not been done because modern-day empire builders (politicians) have found radical Islamic ideology a useful election protectionist tool in the hands of the predominantly Muslim political elite of Northern Nigeria[49].

Together, Boko Haram and Fulani herdsmen atrocities could be staved off or resolved if radicalism, as championed by mainstream Muslim authorities and promoted by the Islamic political class for 'empire-building' in Nigeria, is de-emphasized. Relaxing Islamic conservatism and readjusting the methods to suit the changing realities of the prevailing situation in modern-day Nigeria would help readdress fundamental socio-economic and infrastructural imbalance in the country. The NCEF, in December 2019, implored President Muhammadu Buhari and the Sultan of Sokoto, as Muslims and leaders of Islamic Ummah, to open a dialogue with the rest of the country to resolve the problems caused by religious intolerance in Nigeria[50]. The Christian elders said:

Some Muslim countries in the world are already relaxing their erstwhile hard Islamic stance to operate meaningfully in modern

> *multi-cultural, multi-religious, and multi-ethnic societies. All these are pointers to leaders of the Sunni Muslim Ummah in Nigeria that rigid Islamic intolerance is going out of fashion. It is time for Sunni Muslims in Nigeria, particularly Northern Nigeria, to adjust to modern civilization and restructure the country for the peace, safety, and prosperity of all citizens*[51].

In resolving the constitutional question that would adequately address ethnic overlapping interests, many commentators have vehemently called for the restructuring of Nigeria. As reflected in a 10,335-page draft report of the 2014 National Conference, the restructuring has been touted to be of immense significance to the solution of Nigeria's problem of ethnic domination and rivalries. Kingsley Moghalu, a presidential candidate of the Young Progressives Party (YPP), at the 6th annual conference of the Nigerian Political Science Association (South-east) held at the University of Nigeria, Nsukka on October 29, 2018, delivered an exciting keynote address harping on the importance of restructuring Nigeria to achieve the needed unity and cohesion. According to him,

> *"The problem in our country is that we avoid honest dialogue, which sometimes involves telling ourselves uncomfortable truths. The cries of marginalization, restructuring, and secessionist tendencies are, at their core, a cry for justice in our country. There is no alternative to the Nigerian federation's constitutional re-arrangement if we are to remain one country. Call it "restructuring," "reconfiguration," "redesign," or what you will." Nigeria is not yet a nation. It is a country created by our erstwhile colonial master, the United Kingdom, made up of many ethnic nationalities, but a nation waiting to be born. Given the diversity inherent in our national makeup, the only form of government that can create national unity and cohesion, and enable Nigeria to achieve the promise of its dynamic peoples, is true*

federalism. Such a form of government requires a fundamental overhaul of the 1999 Constitution presently in force to achieve national unity and cohesion as well as the development of the component parts of the federal state at their own pace. Nigeria today is called a "federal republic" but, in reality, is a unitary state. This reality is the result of military intervention in our polity through the first coup of 1966[52].

Gani Adams, who served as the national coordinator of the Oodua Peoples' Congress, also told journalists that he believes in restructuring and would continue to support the call for true federalism. Adams would not conclude without criticizing the 1999 Constitution thus:

I believe that without restructuring, Nigeria cannot move forward. I have been listening to some people talking about constitutional review; what kind of review are they talking about? 26 army officers wrote the constitution. When you see that constitution, you will know that it is a fraud from the beginning[53].

Adams further advocated for the merger of 1960 with 1963 constitutions to achieve true federalism:

We are giving them two options: we are not saying it is a must for them to implement the 2014 national conference (report); we say let us go back to the basics. We have the option of merging 1960 with 1963 constitutions to have a true federation that can easily solve the country's problems[54].

Restructuring could be best understood in terms of Chief Olu Falae, a former Minister of Finance and Secretary to the Government of the Federation (SGF), who was the joint presidential candidate of the All Peoples Party, APP, and Alliance for Democracy, AD in the 1999 election. He was the Head of the Southwest Delegation to the 2014 National Constitutional Conference. Chief Falae, himself a victim of Fulani herdsmen kidnapping, believes restructuring would bring an answer to many of Nigeria's questions. In an interview with Dapo Akinrefon, the Deputy South-West Editor of the Vanguard newspaper, Chief Falae said:

My position has always been that unless we fundamentally restructure Nigeria and return to the kind of arrangement we had at independence, whatever we are doing is a gimmick. The younger people don't know that each region had its own constitution; if you mention it today, they will say you want to break up Nigeria; it is ignorance. As an undergraduate at the university in 1960, in my political science class, which I took along with my economics degree, I studied four constitutional documents. The constitution of Nigeria, the constitution of Western Nigeria, the constitution of Eastern Nigeria, and the constitution of Northern Nigeria. When in 1963, the Mid-West was created out of the Western region, a new constitution was produced. All of these documents were coherent and without any conflict. That was the situation which is not known to most who are in politics today. Every region had its own constitution. So, as far as the regional premiere was concerned, he was not subordinate to the Prime Minister at the center because he had his constitution. Every officer was supreme within the provision of the constitution applicable in his region.

Of course, in order of precedence, the Prime Minister goes before the premiere, but the Prime Minister had no authority to summon the premier and give him instruction. It is not possible because the premier was the head of a regional government. Every region had its constitution, coat of arms, and bearings. Every region had its high commissioner in London; every region was recognized in London as a government. That was how autonomous the regions were, and there was no room for friction. Until and unless we do that, this federation will not know peace and optimum cooperation[55].

In the meantime, since restructuring is proposed as the best solution to Nigeria's recurring violent conflicts, the country has a chance to give it a shot and allow every region to grow based on its resources. Then proceed to develop societal morals according to their socio-cultural and religious worldviews.

Ethnicity is another issue that has bred Nigeria a fair share of trouble, to the extent that it could force the country into inevitable dissolution if not addressed promptly. It has been established that ethnicity is the mother of major problems facing Nigeria, such as insurgency and terrorism. Practical examples of the manifestations of problems associated with ethnicity in Nigeria are evidenced in Kanuri's Boko Haram and Fulani's herdsmen's atrocities. Resolving the problems perpetrated by these armed groups may not be an easy one. While a few still advocate for very decisive actions, preferably military, others have requested that attempts should first be made to call for inter-ethnic conferences in Northern Nigeria to address the issue of terrorism before it boomerangs and eventually swallows the region.

It would be impossible to solve the Fulani herdsmen's violent conflicts if the Boko Haram insurgency is not stamped out in totality. The Fulani herdsmen militancy from every indication seems a calculated response to Boko Haram operations. Consequently, it is not going to be possible to dissolve this menace without tackling it at the root level. This is an urgent call to the Federal Government of Nigeria and all her stakeholders to try as much as possible to quell the Boko Haram crisis in earnest. Once this is done, herdsmen militancy would fizzle out in a similar fashion as it came into existence.

Insurgency and terrorism have done the country a serious disservice. Besides taking a heavy toll on human lives and the destruction of properties, these criminal acts have deepened the food crisis and caused the majority of the nation's population to wallow in poverty and starvation. Northern Nigeria, although acquiring the advantage of political control over the rest of the world, has become a consistent flashpoint of violence where life is harsh, brutish, and short. Indubitably, herdsmen violence has already given birth to trans-border banditry, which has led to the plundering of peoples' properties and reckless killings of hundreds of persons in the Northwest, which is the Fulani's domain. Therefore, it is time for the Fulani power elites to put a final stop to herdsmen terrorism and then address these banditry issues plaguing the region before it balls out of control.

ENDNOTES

CHAPTER ONE

[1]Idris, I. (2018). Livestock and conflict in South Sudan in: K4D Helpdesk Report 484. Brighton, UK: Institute of Development Studies, p2.

[2]ScienceDirect.com.Pastoralism,
http://www.sciencedirect.com/topics/agricultural-and-biological-sciences/pastoralism

[3]Egbuta, U. Understanding the herder-farmer conflict in Nigeria, Social Trend.
htttp://www.accord.org.za/Conflict-Trends/understanding-the-herder-farmer-conflict-in-nigeria/

[4]Wilson, W. (1984). Resources management in a stratified Fulani community (Ph.D.
Desertification), Howard University, 1984.

[5]Davidheisser, M. & Luna, A. (2008). From complementarity to conflict: A historical analysis of
Farmer-Fulbe relations in West Africa, African Journal of Conflict Resolution (8) 1, 81.

[6]Frantz, C. (1975). Pastoral societies, stratification, and national integration in Africa, The
Scandinavian Institute of Africa Studies Research Report (30). Uppsala: Uppsala Offset Centre, 1975, 9.

[7]Waller, R., & Sobania, N.W. (1994). Pastoralism in historical perspective. In Fratkin et al (Eds.).
African Pastoralism Systems: An Integrated Approach. Boulder: Lynne Rienner, p.45 - 68.

[8]van den Brink, R., Bromley, D. & Chavas, J. (1995). The economic of Cain and Abel: Agro-pastoral property rights in the Sahel, The Journal of Development Studies 31 (3), 392.

[9]Ellis, J.E. & D.M. Swift. (1988). Stability of African pastoral ecosystems: Alternate paradigms

and implications for development, Journal of Range Management 41 (6).
[10]Unruh, J.D. (1990). Integration of transhumant pastoralism and irrigated agriculture in semi-arid East Africa, Human Ecology: An Interdisciplinary Journal 18 (3), 224.
[11]Wilson, W. (1984). Resource management in a stratified Fulani community.
[12]Burton, G. (2017). Background report: The Fulani herdsmen https://medium.com/gfburton/background-report-the-fulani-herdsmen-part-i-key-findings-introduction-and-history-383c10f8137c
[13]Ibid.
[14]Ibid.
[15]Southern Kaduna Peoples Union (SOKAPU) Nigeria (2020). A Press Statement released by the
National Public Relations Officer, Luka Binniyat on May 12, 2020
[16]Ibid.
[17]Ibid.
[18]Adamu, A., Alupsen, B. & Gloria, C. (2018). Nigeria: Southern Kaduna and the atrocities of
Hausa-Fulani Muslim Herdsmen (May 2016 - September 2017) 1, in Africa Conflict and
Security Analysis Network (ACSAN). Abuja: World Watch Research, January 10, 2018, 15.
[19]Ibid. pp.15-16
[20]Ibid. p.13.
[21]Benue State Government (2018). A Press Conference Address, Benue State Commissioner for
Information & Orientation, Lawrence Onoja Jnr. Markudi. February 2018.

[22]Human Rights Watch.
https://hrw.org/reports/nigeria040617.htm
[23]Sahara Reporters.com.
www.saharareporters.com/2020/01/28/breaking-pregnant-woman-
16-others-killed-plateau-community-attack-fulani-herdsmen
[24]BBC.Com.
https://www.google.com/amp/s/www.bbc.com/news/amp/world-africa-44597409
[25]Punchng.Com.
https://punchng.com/suspected-herdsmen-kill-13-in-fresh-plateau-attack/%3famp=1
[26]Vanguardngr.Com.
https:www.vanguardngr.com/2020/04/suspected-herdsmen-kill-father-son-one-other-in-ondo-farm/amp/
[27]All Africa.Com.
https://allafrica.com.stories/201907200117.html
[28]Ibid.
[29]Thisdaylive.com.
https://www.thisdaylive.com/index.php/2020/04/26/waiting-for-southeasts-security-outfit/
[30]Vanguardngr.Com.
https:/www.vanguardngr.com/2016/04/bloodbath-enugu-fulani-herdsmen-kill-40/
[31]Ibid.
[32]Guardian.ng.
https://m.guardian.ng/features/focus/living-under-siege-of-herdsmen-in-south-south/
[33]Ibid.

CHAPTER TWO

[1]LEGIT.NG. Origin of Fulani Tribe. https://www.legit-.ng/1776139-historical-origin-fulani-tribe.html
[2]Ibid.
[3]Salamone, F. (2019). Fulani Encyclopedia of World Cultures.https://www.encyclopedia.com/social-sciences-and-law/anthropology-and-archeology/people/fulani
[4]Ibid.
[5]Onwubiko, K.B.C. (1967). History of West Africa (Book One A.D. 1000-1800). Onitsha: Africana Educational Publishers (Nig.), p.183
[6]Ibid.
[7]Ibid.
[8]Ibid.
[9]PULAAKUBLOG.WORDPRESS.COM. Fulani Identity: Pulaaku. https://www.pulaakublog.wordpress.com
[10]Ibid.
[11]Dupire, Marquerite. "Réflexions sur l'ethnicité Peule. Itinérances en pays Peul et ailleurs à la mémoire de P.F. Lacroix, T.2 Literature et Culture, 198, p.169.
[12]PULAAKUBLOG.WORDPRESS.COM. Fulani Identity: Pulaaku. https://www.pulaakublog.wordpress.com
[13]Schareika, N. (2010). Pulaaku in action: Words at work in Wodaabe Clan politics, Ethnology, 49 (3), 220.
[14]PHILOSOPHYBASICS.COM. Zeno of Citium. https://www.philosophybasics.com/philosophers_zeno_citium_html
[15]Ibid.
[16]McKay, B. & McKay, K. (2018). The Spartan way: The mindset and tactics of a battle-ready warrior. https://www.artofmanliness.com/articles/the-spar-

tan-way-the-mindset-and-tactics-of-a-battle-ready-warrior/
[17]Salamone, F. (2019). Fulani, Encyclopedia of World Cultures.https://www.encyclopedia.com/social-sciences-and-law/anthropology-and-archeology/people/fulani
[18]Onwubiko, K.B.C. (1967). History of West Africa (Book One A.D. 1000 - 1800), 203.
[19]Salamone, Frank. https://www.encyclopedia.com/social-sciences-and-law/anthropology-and-archeology/people/fulani
[20]Ibid.
[21]Ibid.
[22]Ibid.
[23]Soriola, E. (2018). History of Fulani herdsmen in Nigeria and today's crisis. https://www.legit.ng/1151632-history-fulani-herdsmen-nigeria-todays-crisis.html
[24]PUNCHNG.COM. Benue Killings: Knocks Over Lawmaker's Comparison of Cow with Human Life. January 27, 2017. http://www.punchng.com/benue-killings-knocks-over-lawmakers-comparison-of-cow-with-human-life/
[25]Ibid.
[26]Ibid.
[27]Hopen, C.E. (1958). The Pastoral Fulbe family in Gwanda. Oxford University Press.
[28]PUNCHNG.COM. Benue Herdsman Commits Suicide Over Death of 200 Cows. Published November 12, 2017. https://punchng.com/benue-herdsman-commits-suicide-over-death-of-200-cow/
[29]Ibid.
[30]Lott, D. & Benjamin H. (1977). Aggressive domination of cattle by Fulani herdsmen and its relation to aggression in Fulani culture and personality, Ethos 5 (2), 184.
[31]Ibid. p. 180
[32]Ibid.

[33]Ibid. p.182.
[34]Ibid.
[35]Ekvall, R.B. (1964). The Tibetan nomadic pastoralists: Structuring of personality and consequences, Wernner-Gren Foundation for Anthropological Research, Symposium 24, 28-29.
[36]Johnson, H.A.S. (1967). The Fulani Empire of Sokoto. Oxford University Press.
[37]Harnischfeger, J. (2006). Islamisation and ethnic conversation in Nigeria, Anthropos 101(1), 37-53.
[38]Ibid.
[39]Ibid.
[40]Ibid.
[41]Hubbard, R. (2014). Religious influence in society, Freedom Magazine (International Edition)
[42]Ibid.
[43]Bugaje, U.M. A Comparative Study of the Movements of Uthman Dan Fodio in Early Nineteenth Century Hausa land and Muhammad Ahmad Al-mahdi in Late Nineteenth Century Sudan. https://www.scribd.com/doc/130117682/A-Comparative-Study-of-the-movements-of-Uthman-Dan-Fodio-in-Early-Nineteenth-Century-Hausaland-and-Muhammad-Ahmad-Al-mahdi-in-Late-Nineteenth-Century)
[44]Levtzion N. & Pouwels R. (2000). The History of Islam in Africa. Ohio University Press.
[45]Ibid.
[46]Adamu, A., Alupsen, B. & Gloria, C. (2018). Nigeria: Southern Kaduna and the atrocities of Hausa-Fulani Muslim Herdsmen (May 2016 - September 2017) 1, in Africa Conflict and Security Analysis Network (ACSAN). Abuja: World Watch

Research, January 10, 2018, 8
[47]Ibid.
[48]Ibid., p.19.
[49]Ibid.
[50]Ibid.
[51]Ferguson, J. (1978). War and Peace in the World's Religions, p.31. New York: Oxford University Press
[52]Churchill, P. (1991). Interpreting the Jihad: Militarism Versus Muslim Pacifism, p. 20. The Acorn.
[53]Adamu, A., Alupsen, B. & Gloria, C. (2018). Nigeria: Southern Kaduna and the atrocities of
Hausa-Fulani Muslim Herdsmen (May 2016 - September 2017) 1, in Africa Conflict and
Security Analysis Network (ACSAN). Abuja: World Watch Research, January 10, 2018, 19.
[54]Sunnewsonline.Com. Insecurity: Miyetti Allah To Roll Out 100000 Vigilantes Across Nigera - Abdullahi Bodejo. June 6, 2020. https://www.sunnewsonline.com/insecurity-miyetti-allah-to-roll-out-100000-vigilantes-across-nigeria-abdullahi-bodejo/
[55]Ubani, Don. Grazing Reserve, Cattle Colony, Takeover of River Banks and RUGA Settlement. July 12, 2019. https://www.thisdaylive.com/index.php/2019/07/12/grazing-reserve-cattle-colony-take-over-of-river-bank-and-ruga-settlement/
[56]Ibid.
[57]Ibid.

CHAPTER THREE

[1]Onwubiko, K.B.C. (1967). History of West of Africa (Book One AD 1000-1800), p. 183, Onitsha: Africa Educational Publishers (Nig.).
[2]Orr, C. (1908). The Hausa race in Journal of the Royal African Society, 7 (27), 278. Oxford University Press.
[3]Onwubiko, K.B.C. (1967). History of West of Africa, p. 40 (Book One AD 1000-1800).
[4]Sule-Kano, A. (2015). The politics of ethnic identity in Nigeria: An examination of the origins of the nations of Hausa-Fulani and Yoruba identities. In Yinusa Kahinde Salami et al (Eds.). Nationalism and Economic JusticeiIn Nigeria, p.490, Ile-Ife: Obafemi Awolowo University Press.
[5]Ibid. pp. 490-491.
[6]Ibid. p. 491.
[7]Ibid.
[8]Robinson, D. (2004). Muslims Societies in African Societies in African History. New York: Cambridge University.
[9]Hunwick, J.O. (1966). The nineteenth century Jihads in Anene, J.C. & G.N. Brown. African in the Nineteenth and Twentieth Centuries, p. 293, Ibadan: Ibadan University Press.
[10]Johnson, A. (2011). The Fulani Jihad and its implication for national integration and development of Nigeria, African Research Review 5(22), 2.
[11]Adeleye, R.A. (1971). Hausaland and Borno. In Ajayi, J.F.A. and M. Crowder (Eds.). History of West Africa, Volume 1 (2nded.)., p. 560, London: Longman Group Ltd.
[12]Ibid., p. 578
[13]Johnson, A. (2011). The Fulani Jihad and its implication for national integration and development of Nigeria, African Research Review 5(22),4.

[14]Adeleye, R.A. (1971). History of West Africa (Vol.1. 2nd edition). London: Longman Group Ltd.,
[15]Johnson, A. (2011). African Research Review 5(22), 4.
[16]Ibid. p.5.
[17]Crowder, M. (1978). The Story of Nigeria, p. 73. London: Faber & Faber.
[18]Aremu, Johnson. October 2011, p.5.
[19]Afe, A. (2003). Political changes in the nineteenth century. In Arifalo, S.A. and G. Ajayi (Eds.). Essays in Contemporary Nigerian History (Vol.1)., p.7 Lagos: First Academic Publishers.
[20]Fage, J.A. (1988). History of Africa (2nd Ed.)., p. 200. London: Unwin Hyman.
[21]Milsome, J.R. (1979). Makers of Nigeria: Usman Dan Fodio. Ibadan: Ibadan University Press Ltd.
[22]Aremu, Johnson. October 2011, p.2.
[23]Ibid. p.7.
[24]Ibid.
[25]Hunwick, J.O. (1966). The nineteenth century Jihads. In Anene, J.C. & G.N. Brown. African in the Nineteenth and Twentieth Centuries, p. 295. Ibadan: Ibadan University Press
[26]Aremu, Johnson. October 2011, p.4.
[27]Crowder, M. (1978). The Story of Nigeria, 73. London: Faber & Faber.
[28]Onwubiko, K.B.C. 1967, p.208.
[29]Ibid. p.209.
[30]Aremu, Johnson. October 2011, p.4.
[31]Onwubiko, K.B.C. 1967, p.207.
[32]Aremu, Johnson. October 2011, p.7.
[33]Milsome, J.R. (1979). Makers of Nigeria: Usman Dan Fodio, 12, 24. Ibadan: Ibadan University Press Ltd,
[34]Isichei, E.A. (1983). A History of Nigeria, p. 207, London:

Longman
[35]Aremu, Johnson. October 2011, p.8.
[36]Hill, M. (2009). The Spread of Islam in West Africa. Stanford: Freeman Spogli Institute for International Studies, Stanford University.
[37]Aremu, Johnson. October 2011, p.9.
[38]Ibid.
[39]Usman, Y.B. (1979). The transformation of political communities: Some notes on significant dimension of the Sokoto Jihad. In Y.B. Usman (Ed.). Studies in the History of Sokoto Caliphate, pp. 34-58.
[40]Aremu, Johnson. October 2011, p.10.
[41]Ikime, O. (1985). In Search of Nigerians: Changing Patterns of Inter-Group Relations in an evolving nation state, Presidential Inaugural Lecture. Nsukka: Historical Society of Nigeria.
[42]Fage, J. A History of Africa, (2nd ed.). London: Unwin Hyman.
[43]Onwubiko, K.B.C. 1967, p.34.
[44]Ibid. pp. 34 -35.
[45]Ibid. pp. 36-37.
[46]Ibid. p.210.
[47]Ibid. 207.
[48]Yusuf, A. (2020, May 23). Muhammad al-Amin al-Kanemi, Daily Trusthttps:www.dailytrust.com.ng/muhammad-al-amin-al-kanemi.html.
[49]Ibid.
[50]Ibid.
[51]Globalsecurity.org. Middle Belt peoples and Languages. https://www.globalsecurity.org/military/world/nigeria/people-middle-belt.htm
[52]Onwubiko, K.B.C. 1967, p.77.

[53]Ibid. p.79.
[54]Ibid.
[55]Ibid.
[56]Ibid.
[57]Dike, K.O. (1962). Origins of the Niger Mission 1841-1891, A paper read at the Centenary of the Mission at Christ Church, Onitsha, on 13 November 1957. Ibadan: Published for the C.M.S. Niger Mission by the Ibadan University Press.
[58]Ibid.
[59]Ibid.
[60]Whitford, J. (1967). Trading Life in Western and Central Africa, p.129.
[61]Ajayi, J.F.A. (1965). Christian Missions in Nigeria 1841-1891: The making of a new elite London: Longman Group Ltd.
[62]Kolapo, F.J. (2005). Making favourable impressions: Bishop Crowther's C.M.S. Niger Mission in Jihadist Nupe Emirate, 1859-1879. In: Korieh, Chima & G. Ugo Nwokeji. Religion, History and Politics in Nigeria: Essays in Honour of Ogbu U. Kalu. Lanham: University Press of America Inc., pp.29-70.
[63]Ibid.
[64]Ibid.
[65]Ibid.
[66]Sudan United Mission. "African Missions, Education and the Road to Independence: The SUM in Nigeria, The Cameroons, Chad, Sudan and Other African Territories." Manuscript Papers from the Centre for the Study of Christianity in the Non-Western World, New College, University of Edinburgh, 1898-1960.
[67]Ibid.
[68]Ibid.
[69]Ibid.
[70]Akinyele, R.T. (2004). Ethnicity, religion and politics in

Nigeria In: Olaniyan, Richard (Ed.). The Amalgamation and Its Enemies: An Interpretative History of Modern Nigeria., p. 129. Ile-Ife: Obafemi Awolowo University Press

[71]Ibid. p.130.

[72]Ibid.

[73]Akinyele, R.T. (1990). States creation and boundary adjustments in Nigeria: A study in the approach to the problems of ethnic minority groups in Nigeria, 1900-1987 [Unpublished Ph.D. Thesis] University of Lagos.

CHAPTER FOUR

[1]Akpan, U (2019). Ikono The Cradle of Ibibio Nation: A Refutation. Uyo: Heritage Preservation
Foundation, 79.
[2]Akpan, O. (2004). The evolution of the Nigerian State: Pre-colonial to independence period. In
Akpan Akpan & Oluwabamide, Abiodun (Eds). Nigerians and their cultural heritage. Lagos: Lisjohnson Resources Publishers, pp. 13-14.
[3]Onwubiko, K.B.C. (1967). History of West Africa (Book One A.D. 1000-1800). Onitsha: Africana
Educational Publishers (Nig.), p.183
[4]Ibid., p.187
[5]Ibid.
[6]Akpan, O. (2004). The evolution of the Nigerian State: Pre-colonial to independence period. In
Akpan Akpan & Oluwabamide, Abiodun (Eds). Nigerians and their cultural heritage. Lagos: Lisjohnson Resources Publishers, pp. 13-14.
[7]Ibid., p.15.
[8]Ikime, O. (1982). The Fall of Nigeria: The British Conquest. London: Heinemann Books, 7.
[9]Historyworld.Net. History of Nigeria. http://historyworld.net/wrldhis/PlainTextHistoriesResponsive.asp?historyid=ad41
[10]Ibid.
[11]Akpan, O. (2004). The evolution of the Nigerian State: Pre-colonial to independence period.
In Akpan Akpan & Oluwabamide, Abiodun (Eds). Nigerians and their cultural heritage.

Lagos: Lisjohnson Resources Publishers, pp. 13-14.
[12]Burns, A.A. (1958). History of Nigeria. London: Faber & Faber, 64.
[13]Akpan, Otoabasi, 2004, p.16.
[14]Arikpo, O. (1967). The Development of Modern Nigeria. London: Longman Press, 9.
[15]Perham, M. (1960). Lugard: The Years of Authority, 1899-1945. London: Oxford University Press, p.45.
[16]Akpan, Otoabasi, 2004, p.17.
[17]Ibid., p.18.
[18]Ibid.
[19]Davidheisser, M. & Luna, A. (2008). From complementarity to conflict: A historical analysis of Farmer-Fulbe relations in West Africa, African Journal of Conflict Resolution (8) 1, 81.
[20]Elliswood, W. (1995). Nomads at the Crossroads. New Internationalist, 266. http://www.newint.org/issue266/keynote.htm
[21]Waller, R., & Sobania, N.W. (1994). Pastoralism in historical perspective. In Fratkin et al (Eds.). African Pastoralism Systems: An Integrated Approach. Boulder: Lynne Rienner, p.45.
[22]Omuojine, E.O. (1999). The land use act and the English Doctrine of Estate in Journal of the Institution of Estate Surveyors and Valuers, 22 (3), 45.
[23]Udoekanem, N (2014). Land ownership in Nigeria: Historical development, current issues and future expectations in Journal of Environmental and Earth Science 4 (21),183.

[24]Ibid, p.183.
[25]Ibid.
[26]Ibid., p.185.
[27]Iro, I. Grazing reserve development: A panacea to the intractable strife between farmers and
herders. Gamji.com. www.gamji.com/fulani8.htm
[28]Frantz, C. (1981). Fulbe continuity and change under Five Flags Atop West Africa:
Territoriality, ethnicity stratification and national integration, Change and Development
in Nomadic and Pastoral Societies. Netherlands: E.J. Brills, 1981, 89-115.
[29]Awogbade, M.O. "Livestock Development and Range Use in Nigeria" in: The Future of Pastoral People: Proceedings of a Conference held in Institute of Development Studies, Nairobi, August 4-8 1980.
[30]Iro, Ismail. Gamji.com. www.gamji.com/fulani8.htm
[31]Bello, Muhammed (2015). How to solve the Fulani herdsmen versus farmers clashes in
Nigeria, MIYETTI Allah, Premium Times Online Newspaper, 14th October, 2015
https://www.premium-times-ng.com.html
Endnotes
[32]Pastoral Editorial. Implementing State's Anti-Open Grazing Laws. <https://punchng.com/implemeting-states-anti-open-grazing-laws/
[33]Duru, Peter (2018). Herdsmen killings: Our problem with Miyetti Allah has just deepened –
Benue Tribal Leaders. https://www.vanguardngr.com/2018/06/herdsmen-killings-
problem-miyetti-allah-just-deepened-benue-tribal-leaders/

[34]Ibid.
[35]Ibid.
[36]Ibid.
[37]Sunday, O. (2018). Nigeria's cattle colony' problem: Why a controversial policy proposed by the Nigerian Government will not resolve land disputes in Nigeria. Aljazeera.com, February 8, 2018. https:www.aljzaeera.com/indepth/opinion/nigeria-cattle-colony-problem-1801281046454550.html
[38]Toroma, S. (2019). 7 things you should know about Buhari's controversial RUGA settlements. Pulse.ng, July 1, 2019. https:www.pulse.ng/news/local/ruga-7-things-to-know-about buharis-controversial-settlements-/tcjmr7m
[39]Ibid.
[40]Lawrence, N., Terhemba, D., Ayodele, A., Daniel, A., Anietie, A. & Joseph, L. (2019). More states, groups reject Ruga Settlements for Herders. Guardian.ng, July 2, 2019 https://www.m.guardian.ng/news/more-states-groups-reject-ruga-settlements-for-herders/
[41]Ibid.
[42]Ibid.
[43]Ibid.
[44]Danmole, H.O. (1990). Religion and politics in Colonial Northern Nigeria: The case of Ilorin Emirate, Journal of Religious History, 16 (2), 140.
[45]Ikime, O. (1970). The establishment of indirect rule in Nigeria. Tarikh, 3, 1-15.
[46]James, P. (2017). A review of the secularity of the Nigerian Constitution, The Cable,

September 30, 2017. https://www.thecable.ng/review-secular-ity-nigerian-1999-constitution
[47]Marshall, P. (2005). Nigeria: Shari'a in a fragmented country, Radical Islam's Rules. Lanham:
MD: Roman & Littlefield, 114.
[48]Ibid., p.115.
[49]Demarest, L., Langer, A. & Ukiwo, U. (2020). Nigeria's Federal Character Commission (FCC): A
critical appraisal, Oxford Development Studies, doi: 10.1080/13600818.2020.1727427
[50]Omokhunu, G. (2019). Christian elders to Buhari, Sultan: Let's build united country, forum
wants democracy as national ideology, The Nation 13 (4899), 1-6.
[51]Omokhunu, G. (2019). How to restore security, Middle belt forum, The Nation, Thursday 20th
June, 30.
[52]Ibid.

CHAPTER FIVE

[1]Mambula, M.A. (2016). Nigeria: Ethno-religious and Socio-political violence and pacifism In Northern Nigeria. New York: Page Publishing Incorporation
[2]Ibid.
[3]Ibid.
[4]Sampson, I. (2012). Religious violence in Nigeria: Causal diagnoses and strategic recommendations to the State and religious communities, Accord. https://www.accord.org.za/a-jcr-issues/religious-violence-in-nigeria/
[5]Ibid.
[6]Barkindo, A. (2016, October 11). Nigerian Fulani herdsmen's attacks continue amidst government inaction. Worldwatch Monitor. https://www.worldwatchmonitor.org/2016/10/nigerian-fulani-herdsmens-attacks-continue-amidst-government-inaction/
[7]Akinyetun, T. (2016). Staff to gun: Herdsmen in Nigeria, Asian Journal of Multidisciplinary Studies, 4 (8), 39.
8Ibid.
[9]Aljazeera.Com. Nigeria Rejects Boko Haram 'Caliphate' Claim. Published on August 24, 2014. <https://www.aljazeera.com/news/africa/2014/08/nigeria-rejects-boko-haram-caliphate-claim-20148251062176395.html
[10]The Pivot Newspaper (Vol.1, No.8), May 30, 2011, p.3.
[11]Ibid.
[12]Burton, John. (2017). Background report: The Fulani herdsmen (Part 1 - Key findings,
introduction, and history in Project Cyma. https://www/medium.com/@gfburton/background-report-the-fulani-herdsmen-part-i-key-findings

[13]Teniola, E. (2019, May 22). The influence of the Kanuri on Buhari. PM News. May, 2019.
https://www.pmnewsnigeria.com/2019/05/22/the-influence-of-the-kanuri-on-buhari-by-eric-teniola/

[14]Ibid.

[15]Pointblanknews.com. Buhari's plot to hand over power to Kanuris meets stiff resistance from fellow Fulanis: Triggers clashes on road to 2019. Published on April 9, 2017.
<https://pointblanknews.com/pbn/exclusive/buharis-plot-hand-power-kanuris-meets-stiff-resistance-fellow-fulanis-triggers-clashes-road-2019/

[16]Ibid.

[17]Ibid.

[18]Ibid.

[19]Leadership Newspaper. (2020, July 9). Power play in EFCC as Director of Operations, Umar,
takes over, 6.

CHAPTER SIX

[1]Akinyele, R.T. (2004). Ethnicity, religion and politics in Nigeria In Olaniyan, Richard (ed.). The amalgamation and its enemies: An Interpretative History of Modern Nigeria. P. 123. Ile-Ife: Obafemi Awolowo University Press.
[2]Crowder, M. (1978). The Story of Nigeria London: Faber & Faber.
[3]Hale, H.E. (2008). The foundations of ethnic politics: Separatism of states and nations In Eurasia and the world. Cambridge, UK: Cambridge University Press.
[4]Sule-Kano, A. (2015). The politics of ethnic identity in Nigeria: An examination of the origins of the notions of the Hausa-Fulani and the Yoruba identities In Yinusa Kehinde et al. Nationalism and economic justice in Nigeria, p. 487. Ile-Ife: Obafemi Awolowo University Press.
[5]Ibid., p.503.
[6]Cohen, R. (1978). Ethnicity: Problems and focus in anthropology, Annual Review of Anthropology, 7.
[7]Dahiru, M. (2020). Boko Haram war without end, The Sun Newspaper, 16 (4458).
[8]Muller, J.Z. (2008). Us and them in Current Issue (501), March/April 2008, pp.9-14.
[9]Aluko, M.A.O. & Ajani, O.A. 2009). Ethnic nationalism and the Nigerian democratic experience in the fourth republic, African Research Review: An International Multi-Disciplinary Journal 3 (1), 486.
[10]Ibid., p. 485.

[11]Nkolika, O. E. (2007). Citizenship and ethnic militia politics in Nigeria - Marginalization or
identity question? The case of MASSOB. Being a Paper Presented At the 3rd Global Conference On Pluralism, Inclusion and Citizenship, at Salzburg, Austria on November 18th - 19th, 2007.

[12]Alabelewe, A. (2017, July 16). Southern Kaduna: Blame FG, foreign herdsmen - Miyetti Allah,
The Nation Newspaper, p.8.

[13]Ibid.

[14]Ibid.

[15]Ibid.

[16]Ibid.

[17]Ibid.

[18]Egbiri, K., Chido, O., Neme, S., Egbejule, M. & Inemesit, A. (2020, February 19). Living under
siege of herdsmen in South-South, The Guardian. https://m.guardian.ng/features/focus/living-under-siege-of-herdsmen-in-south-south/

[19]Ibid.

[20]Omokhunu, G. (2019, June 20). How to restore security, by Middle Belt Forum, The Nation Newspaper, p.30.

[21]Amalu, G. (2019, May 28). Unlawful arms, The Nation Newspaper, p.20.

[22]Ibid.

[23]Ibid.

[24]Ibid.

[25]The Nation Newspaper. (2020, March 19). Residents flee as herdsmen take over Benue Community, p.4.

[26]Amalu, G. (2019, May 28) The Nation Newspaper, p.20.

[27]Ibid.

[28]Punch Editorial Board (2018, January 23). Disarming

AK-47s bearing Fulani herdsmen The Punchng.com, https://punchng.com/disarming-ak-47s-bearing-fulani-herdsmen/

[29]Ibid.

[30]Asadu, C. (2020, March 4). Ohanaeze to IGP: Police silent while herdsmen carry AK-47 rifles in Anambra https://www.thecable.ng/ohanaeze-to-igp-police-silent-while-herdsmen-carry-ak-47-rifles-in-anambra

[31]Ibid.

[32]Ibid.

[33]Ibid.

[34]Ibid.

[35]Ibrahim, R., Elekwa, E., Onogu, S., Adedeji, T. & Jimoh, A. (2020). Nnamdi Kanu, Youth Council others back Amotekun, The Nation Newspaper, 3 (4917), 2-3.

[36]Alli, Y. (2019, July 20). Obasanjo obsessed with national conference - Yari: says new confab unnecessary, faults stigmatization of Fulani, The Nation Newspaper, p.44.

[37]Ibrahim, R., Elekwa, E., Onogu, S., Adedeji, T. & Jimoh, A. (2020). Nnamdi Kanu, Youth Council others back Amotekun, The Nation Newspaper, 3 (4917), 2-3.

[38]Oyedele, O. (2020, January 17). Western Nigeria security network: Malami got it wrong, The Nation Newspaper, p.18.

[39]Adams, G. (2020, January 17). Letter to Minister Malami, The Nation Newspaper, p.3.

[40]Ibid.

[41]Ibrahim, R., Elekwa, E., Onogu, S., Adedeji, T. & Jimoh, A. (2020). Nnamdi Kanu, Youth Council others back Amotekun, The Nation Newspaper, 3 (4917), 2-3.

[42]Ibid.

[43]Ibid.

[44]Ibid., p.2.

[45]Ahon, F. (2020, March 6). South-South Governors to set up regional security outfit, Vanguard, https://www.vanguardngr.com/2020/03/south-south-governors-to-set-up-regional-security-outfit/

[46]Ojiabor, O., Onogu, S., & Akowe, T. (2020, January 17). Fayemi: Amotekun aligns with Buhari's vision, Nation Newspaper, pp.7-8.

[47]Omokhunu, G. (2019). Christian elders to Buhari, Sultan: Let's build united country, forum wants democracy as national ideology, The Nation, 13(4899), pp.1-6.

[48]Adesomoju, A. (2020, June 22). Fasoranti, Clarke, Nwodo, 13 others sue Buhari over lopsided appointments, Punch, https://punchng.com/breaking-fasoranti-clarke-nwodo-13-others-sue-buhari-over-lopsided-appointments/

[49]Dahiru, M. (2020, May 27). Boko Haram war without end, The Sun Newspaper.

[50]Omokhunu, G. (2019). The Nation, pp.1-6.

[51]Ibid.

[52]Moghalu, K. (2018, October 29). How to restructure Nigeria: Why, what, how and when? Being a keynote address delivered by Moghalu, presidential candidate of the Young Progressives Party (YPP), at the 6th annual conference of the Nigerian Political Science Association (South-east) at the University of Nigeria, Nsukka https://www.thecable.ng/how-to-restructure-nigeria-why-what-how-and-when

[53]Makinde, F. & Dada, P. (2017, December 29). Adams visits Aregbesola, Afenifere, backs Restructuring, Punch, https://punchng.com/adams-visits-aregbesho-

la-afenifere-backs-restruturing/
[54]Ibid.
[55]Akinrefon, D. (2020, July 13). 2023: Restructuring, not zoning will solve Nigeria's problems – Olu Falae, Vanguard, https://www.vanguardngr.com/2020/07/2023-restructuring-not-zoning-will-solve-nigerias-problems-olu-falae/

There has been a long history of conflicts between cattle herdsmen and farmers in Nigeria. A shift in the character of this historical crisis has been seen in the time since 2015. Scholars world over have been wondering if this crisis in any way draws inspiration from the Boko Haram insurgency waged since 2009. Some, on the other hand, ponder if this is a camouflage agenda aimed at wiping out non-Islamic populations in order to gain more grazing land to spread Islam to the territories conquered. This puzzle has more to it than you think.

www.ingramcontent.com/pod-product-compliance
Ingram Content Group UK Ltd.
Pitfield, Milton Keynes, MK11 3LW, UK
UKHW020226250726
13967UKWH00001B/214

9 780578 811833